# Solidarity With Victims

Matthew L. Lamb

# SOLIDARITY WITH VICTIMS

## Toward a Theology
## of Social Transformation

CROSSROAD · NEW YORK

1982

The Crossroad Publishing Company
575 Lexington Avenue, New York, NY 10022

Copyright © 1982 by Matthew L. Lamb

Printed in the United States of America

*Library of Congress Cataloging in Publication Data*

Lamb, Matthew L.
   Solidarity with victims.

   Includes index.
   1. Sociology, Christian.   I. Title.
BT738.L253          261.1          81-22145
ISBN 0-8245-0471-2                 AACR2

Chapter 2, "Critical Theory and the End of Intellectual Innocence," ap-
peared in an earlier form as "The Challenge of Critical Theory," in *Sociology
and Human Destiny*, edited by Gregory Baum, copyright 1980 by Gregory
Baum, and published by The Seabury Press. This material is used by permis-
sion of The Seabury Press.

Dedicated
to
the many victims of oppression
in
El Salvador, Guatemala, Honduras;
especially to those
priests, nuns, and missionaries who,
like Archbishop Oscar Romero,
were martyred for their following of
Jesus Christ
in his identification of God
with the many struggles of victims
everywhere

# Contents

# Preface

Trying to understand history in self-critical solidarity with the many victims of sexism, racism, economic exploitation, militarism, and environmental pollution leaves little room for the more comfortable alternatives of optimism and pessimism. Optimism tends to trivialize their sufferings with easy assurances of better and brighter tomorrows. Are the victims of history condemned to die in the waiting rooms of ever more illusory futures? Pessimism tends to romanticize the suffering with dark forebodings of some impending doom. Do victims struggle to transcend their sufferings only to enter a cynical world of meaningless catastrophe? Optimism and pessimism ignore the victims and concentrate more on the victors of history. They differ profoundly from hope and critical realism which motivate victims to overcome their sufferings.

Solidarity with victims is an imperative for responsible theology today. Such solidarity is self-critical. For it means much more than an optimist's sympathy for "the less fortunate," or a pessimist's collectivity as though, in the words of G. K. Chesterton, the victims "were physically stuck together like dates in a grocer's shop." Self-critical solidarity means, to paraphrase John Paul II's recent encyclical *On Human Work*, communities *of* victims and *with* the victims in common reflection and action "against the degradation of human beings preventing them from becoming the rightful subjects or agents of their own labor and history." Movements of solidarity, John Paul II reminds us, must always be open to dialogue and collaboration with others. The hope and critical realism of the victims are especially needed by intellectuals and theologians today when the tendencies to superficial optimism and false pessimism are so strong. Modernity

began with optimistic celebrations of pure reason embodied in
the burgeoning sciences, technologies, and industries. Capitalism and communism draw upon such optimism in inevitable
human progress. Confronted, however, with the many victims of
this progress, optimism quickly turns into a pessimism resigned
to totalitarian controls. Naively innocent optimism in pure reason becomes a pessimistic litany of irrationality and death as it
views the victims of so many local and world wars, spreading
disease and starvation, widening gaps between rich and poor,
environmental pollutions, and the trillions of dollars poured into
seemingly endless series of arms races. Rather than empowering
victims to transcend their sufferings, such optimism turned pessimism would literally destroy the very possibility of life on this
planet.

Theologians should be attuned to how such ceremonies of innocence can turn into litanies of death. After all, religion lost its
innocence long ago. Its crusades, wars, and bigotry occasioned
modernity's quest for the purity of reason. Now that pure reason
has brought us even more victims than the old impure religion,
we can no longer responsibly practice reason or religion without
self-critical solidarity with the victims of both. Only their hope
and critical realism will empower us to avoid the illusions of optimism and pessimism. This book is a programmatic study of
some of the changes required if we are to do theology in self-critical solidarity with victims. It analyzes some of the methodological tasks which such a political theology must undertake if it is
to contribute to genuine social transformation. The chapters,
some of which have been published before and are modified
here, are not meant to offer a finished theology of social transformation. They are addressed to theological communities and
colleagues in the hope of contributing, however modestly, to the
ongoing discussions of how we should change the ways in which
we do theology in order to mediate more transformatively the
significance of our religious traditions to the social and political
issues of today.

I wish to express my gratitude to those who have continued to
help with their comments and criticisms. The faculty, students,
and community organizers who regularly participate in our

Catholic Worker Institute meetings at Marquette University, especially the communities at Casa Maria and McKinley House, along with Lucy Edelbeck, Marc Ellis, Jean and Michael Fleet, Howard Fuller, Roberto and Michelle Goizueta, William and Judith Kelsey, Joyce Little, Daniel and Marjorie Maguire, William Miller, Sebastian Moore, Joseph O'Malley, and Karen Wilhelmy. I still have much to learn from their concerns and commitments, as well as those of other students and faculty who participate in the feminist community, Leaven, the Educational Opportunity Program, the Multi-Racial Justice Community, and the Central American Solidarity Coalition in Milwaukee. The same applies to my friends and colleagues elsewhere, especially Gregory Baum, Elizabeth and Francis Schüssler Fiorenza, Robert Doran, Fred Lawrence, Bernard Lonergan, Johann B. Metz, William Shea, and David Tracy. Finally, I wish to express my admiration and gratitude to The Catholic Foreign Mission Society of America, or Maryknoll, for their assistance in providing me with a Walsh-Price Fellowship and, more importantly, for the genuine Catholicity of their solidarity with the victims of history.

Matthew L. Lamb
*Marquette University*
*Milwaukee, Wisconsin*

# Introduction

This book tries to discern the outlines of a practice of reason and of religion in a self-critical solidarity with the victims of history. Only in such a solidarity will religion and reason stop posturing foolishly. Honest questions, however humbling, are the matrix of liberating insights. Confession and conversion are as good for the mind as they are for the soul. There are hopeful stirrings in theology. Theology is—as it always has been—a precarious balancing act with one foot in religion (*theos*) and the other in reason (*logos*). The first chapter sketches the wreckage of our anguished world and the honest efforts of liberation theologies to respond prophetically to the victims of its many sins. Faith as genuine is a knowledge born of love, and the agapic praxis, or love lived in solidarity with victims struggling to overcome their suffering, is the heart of liberation theologies. Political theologies are the efforts to mediate to reason the commitments of such a heart.

The second chapter explores such a mediation. Liberation theologies unmask the pretense of "pure religion." The practice of religion is not exempt from the social sins dehumanizing life on this planet. Religion involves us in a continuing practical conversion or *metanoia* as a repentant withdrawal or exodus from evil. There is a parallel movement within philosophy in the critical theory of the Frankfurt School of Social Research. Critical theory unmasks the pretense of "pure reason." The practice of reason involves its own forms of conversion as a continual withdrawal from the deformations masquerading as reason. Reason is essentially practical as reason yet to be realized in history and society. The importance of this task can be intimated by paraphrasing recent works by two noted American historians:

the dialectic of Enlightenment can disclose how, if Europe imagined and America realized the Enlightenment, America was fated to twist the empire of reason into the reason of empire.[1] Critical theory cannot provide a completely adequate framework for all sociological analysis, and my discussion of it should not be so interpreted. Rather I find it one of the strongest sociological traditions in emphasizing the need for criticizing the many forms of instrumental rationality.

The third chapter provides an overview of the relationships between theory and praxis in contemporary Christian theologies. In some respects it is a discernment of theological spirits. I distinguish five models or paradigms. To use a metaphor referred to above, one might say that theologians in the first model cling to the notion that pure religion is still possible, theologians in the second model hope that some form of pure practical reason can still be found, theologians in the third model strive to accentuate divine transcendence, while theologians in the final two models spell out the implications of such a transcendence in the sense of either a theoretical (fourth) or practical (fifth) acceptance of the need for confession and conversion on the part of both religion and reason.

The fourth chapter articulates some of the categories required in a socially critical reconstruction of church teachings or dogmas. Classical orthodoxy expresses subversive memories linked to eschatological and apocalyptic expectations of the coming reign of God. As such they are more than just expressions of the plausibility structures of the cultures in which they emerged—as the old liberal discussions of the hellenization of Christianity maintained. Orthodoxy contains traditions too valuable to be left to the prejudices of fundamentalist, Moral Majority types. Dogma tends to be a harsh word in modernity, full of pejorative connotations, while almost everyone praises experience. Advertising pushes new products promising ever richer experiences—experiences which the myriad victims of instrumental rationality and its cultural offspring, middle-class consumerism, cannot buy. The harsh *anathema sit* of classical dogmas can be deprivatized and related to those religious imperatives which call for changes of heart and conduct capable of redeeming human life so endangered by the modern fetishism of commodity-experience.

The final chapter takes up the themes of the previous ones in the context of a programmatic discussion of how theology can be done now that the ages of religious and rational innocence have passed. I indicate how Johann B. Metz faced this issue in regard to the transcendental theology of Karl Rahner. This issue is then discussed with reference to the work of Bernard Lonergan in laying the foundations for a dialectical retrieval of those aspirations of religion and of reason so crucial to the task of honestly engaging theology in the collaborative labors of a postmodern social transformation.[2]

## NOTES

1. Cf. Henry S. Commager, *The Empire of Reason: How Europe Imagined and America Realized the Enlightenment* (New York: Doubleday, 1978); William A. Williams, *Empire as a Way of Life* (New York: Oxford University Press, 1980). The subtitle of Professor Williams's book is: "An Essay on the Causes and Character of America's Present Predicament along with a Few Thoughts about an Alternative."

2. For largely complementary retrievals of those traditions of moral reflection so important for such a postmodern transformation, cf. Alasdair MacIntyre, *After Virtue* (Notre Dame, Ind.: University of Notre Dame Press, 1981), and Gibson Winter, *Liberating Creation* (New York: Crossroad, 1981).

# Chapter 1

# Social Sin and Social Transformation

## The Tasks of Prophetic and Political Theologies

**V**ox victimarum vox Dei—the cries of victims are the voice of God. The scandal of the Cross is the scandal of God identified with all the victims of history in the passion of Christ. That identification was not a passive acceptance of suffering but an empowering transformation whereby the forces of death and evil were overcome through the resurrection. This empowering transformation was not an isolated, individual event cut off from the rest of human history. It was an event the meaning of which challenges those who believe to engage in a discipleship of faith, hope, and love. The discipleship is a life lived in a dying identification with the victims. Prophecy is constituted by an agapic life or praxis whereby the cries of victims are articulated into a voice protesting the victimization of humans by other humans. Political theologies seek to translate such an agapic, prophetic voice into the terms and categories of the mind through a noetic praxis. If prophetic theologies are the narratives of the heart open to the cries of victims, political theologies are the efforts of the mind seeking to understand the reasons of such a heart.

The empowering transformation through the resurrection overcame the forces of death and evil in a manner which liberated human freedom. Redemption was not an overpowering of human freedom, as though divine omnipotence would cancel out the forces of death and evil by imposing a humane order upon human history. The reign of God prophetically incarnated in the resurrection-event was not the act of a divine engineer controlling human history to bring about the best of all possible worlds in spite of human response. Empowering transformation through a divine identification with the victims of history did not "produce" a redeemed humankind the way a factory produces consumer objects. That would be a contradiction in terms, for the victims of history are what they are precisely by such an effort to dominate and control. Empowering transformation is an invitation, a call or imperative, to live out (praxis) God's identification with the victims of history through personal and social conversion, or *metanoia.*

This chapter will explore this understanding of redemption as an empowering transformation by discussing how social sin is constitutive of an anguished world, how prophetic theologies are engaged in an agapic praxis aimed at counteracting those sins, the tasks of political theologies in mediating the values of such an agapic praxis to human intelligence; and, finally, will conclude with some of the main projects which political theology in North America should undertake.

### Social Sin and an Anguished World

During the eighteenth and nineteenth centuries there was a strong tendency to understand "an anguished world" differently than we do today. The histories of human suffering which seemed to provoke passionate concern in the previous two centuries centered more around those resulting from the jeopardy of human life confronted with natural disasters. In 1756 Voltaire's eloquent denunciation of needless suffering was occasioned by the Lisbon earthquake of the previous year. A hundred years later Comte's eulogy of positive science implemented in technology and industry promised a control of nature which would put an end to disease, plague, famine, and floods by subordinating all the positive sciences and their implementations in industry to the advancement and progress of human life.[1] Darwin's discoveries were soon extrapolated into a social Darwinism which interpreted human progress as a struggle for survival against hostile environments. Where the seventeenth century had taken refuge in the laws of nature discovered by empirical science as embodying a reason over against the whims of religious authoritarianism, by the nineteenth century science had become humanity's weapon in defense against hostile natural processes.[2] So strong was this faith in natural science that even when Marx and Freud shifted the burdens of human suffering from nature to history, they still felt compelled to cast their insights in the guise of new domains of natural science.[3] Marx wrote in 1861: "Darwin's book is very important and serves me as a basis in natural science for the class struggle in history."[4] Freud's hope to reduce psychic energy to physical energy also tended to "interiorize" conflict in terms of the struggles between id and superego.[5]

The last eight decades have profoundly changed the understanding of "an anguished world." Increasingly, the anguish in the world has been shifted from the weary shoulders of mother nature to the proud shoulders of a male-dominated history so aptly symbolized by Atlas. Anguish has taken an anthropocentric (indeed, androcentric) turn to the subject. The countless wars and the nuclear arms race are only more evident symptoms of this turn. Never before in human history have so many humans slaughtered their fellow human beings on such a massive scale.[6] The Lisbon earthquake pales in comparison with Hiroshima and Nagasaki. Famines and plagues can hardly measure up to the demonic intensity of the holocaust. The terrors of nature have tended to take a back seat to the horrors of history. This shift from a primacy of nature to a primacy of history as the locus of human suffering has led to a recovery of a "deprivatized" notion of human perversity. The Cartesian emphasis upon human subjectivity as an isolated *ego cogito* had parallels in moral teachings which stressed the private and individualistic character of evil acts or sins.[7] History as a realm of freedom over against nature seemed to hold the promise of overcoming natural and human evils through the progress of science and education. Now, however, we realize how these very means of human emancipation can be—and, to a great extent, have been—twisted into even more horrible forms of dehumanization and oppression. Individuals may have the best will in the world, may be good and upright, and yet by their actions contribute to social and historical processes which oppress and dehumanize. There is a pathological distortion of human existence—a tendency to distort life into death and good into evil. Paul Ricoeur refers to this as *la faute* and Bernard Lonergan terms it "bias."[8] Religious symbols and narratives of "fall" and "sin" can now be understood in social and historical or ontological perspectives.

The social sins—or biases—of economic oppression, racism, ecological pollution, and sexism stain human history with their all too evident horrors. Indeed, the very means which previously were cultivated to promote human emancipation—science and technology—are increasingly seen as perverted by a necrophilic bias. By some estimates almost half of all the natural scientists in First World countries are engaged in military related research. Planetary suicide is, as Sartre and the *Bulletin of Atomic Scientists* remind us, not only a possibility but an increasing probability. Now natural disasters themselves tend to be understood as resulting from human blindness and bias. Ivan Illich claims that the major diseases afflicting industrialized societies are iatrogenic in origin.[9] Diseases in developing countries are intensified by the displacement of capital for industrial and military expansion. World hunger—as the studies of Frances M. Lappé, Joseph Collins, and Susan George, among others, demonstrate—is not the natural result of too many people and too few resources but is quite literally man-made (whenever I use "man" I refer to male predominance) in terms of world trade patterns, multinational agribusiness biased toward maximizing its assets, and inequitable land distribution. Even such tragic famines as in the Sahel or in Bangladesh show how we cannot blame nature so much as the human modernization of hunger.[10]

Where Adam Smith and others saw poverty resulting from the combination of a human lack of industriousness and scarcity of natural resources, a whole battery of contemporary studies from such diverse sources as the United Nations, Reports to the Club of Rome, the Institute for Policy Study, and so on, indicates how the global dimensions of poverty are endemic or systematically intrinsic to the present patterns of macroeconomic accumulation and distribution. Indeed, the so-called solutions now being offered to world poverty from *both* late capitalist *and* state socialist perspectives are increasingly seen as counsels of despair by those truly interested in a new world economic order.[11] For both late capitalism and state socialism substitute various forms of political/economic regimentation to bolster up their ignorance of the dynamic interaction of macroeconomic phases of surplus accumulation and basic distribution. Marx, it should be subversively remembered, attempted a *critique* of political economy.[12] Poverty is man-made, and its present global intensification results more from human stupidity and a shortsighted bias of unenlightened self-interest than it does from a cunningly intelligent greed. As I have pointed out elsewhere, late capitalism is an ignorantly bad materialization of idealism, and state socialism is an ignorantly bad idealization of materialism. The massive economic exploitation which has and is crucifying millions upon millions of human beings is *condemned* by an echo from the past: "Forgive them for they know not what they do." Any economic system which intensifies poverty is not only immoral but also profoundly stupid.[13]

Racism is rooted in group bias. Such bias feeds upon the naive empiricism which judges peoples by superficial differences in skin pigmentation or ethnic origins. As such, racism has for ages provided the biased excuse for exploitation and slavery. In the last few centuries (and for many ideologues left over from that past), racial differences were blamed on inherently qualitative differences caused by nature. Religious and academic "theorists" of the calibre of Joseph Arthur, Houston S. Chamberlain, or Alfred Rosenberg were—and perhaps in the guise of Benoist or Wilson still are—there to provide biased rationalizations for colonial exploitation and degradation. South Africa brutally reminds us of how much that past is still our present; and how much more refined and subtly demonic racism has become in the exchange economies of the twentieth century. Race and ethnicity are cleverly manipulated in order to divide the have-nots, as they compete for jobs and the welfare crumbs doled out by impersonal bureaucracies. Welfarism is colonialism *ad intra* (within the nation-states). No, we cannot blame nature for racism. It too is man-made. What countless histories of human suffering have and are destroying millions of people because they are black, brown, yellow, red, gray, Jewish, Palestinian, Hispanic . . . the list goes on as group bias eats at the heart of our humanity.[14]

So strongly has an anguished world turned from nature to history that now the very tools of science and technology which were supposed to save us from the terrors of nature are, through industrialization, polluting and destroying environment after environment. Nature, as Hegel observed, is being sucked up into history. But Hegel hardly envisaged the megamachine of modern industry which would turn nature into a resource reservoir feeding the rapacious appetite of the megamachine, and into a dumping site where the machine would spew its toxic wastes. While we still are filled with awe at a volcanic eruption like Mount St. Helens, the effects of such natural disasters on the environment and atmosphere are dwarfed when compared to the day-in, day-out pollutions of the megamachine. Yes, nature is increasingly being sucked up into history. But history is radically distorted by bias. And in this process the bias is a hubris which threatens to destroy the natural basis for human life on this planet. There are limits to how long nature can be dominated by the man-made megamachine. Whom the gods will destroy they first make blind.[15]

Little wonder, then, that our century would witness a growing protest of feminism against the blind rage of sexism which runs like a deep morally biased fault throughout human history. If the bias runs deep in the caverns of the human psyche, the social distortions and alienations of male-female relationships are all too plain for those with eyes to see. Nor is the depth of the bias in the male psyche a product of nature—as psychologists and anthropologists unaware of their own androcentric bias have often maintained.[16] Indeed, a feminist correction of Jung's anima-animus orientations of the human psyche indicates how these orientations are present in both males and females. The widespread repression of anima in males (and correlative oppression of animus in females) results more from historical processes of socialization and enculturation in patriarchically or androcentrically biased societies.[17] Here, as in the other forms of bias mentioned above, one is staggered by the overwhelming evidence of anguished human suffering resulting from bias in our historical world. Millions upon millions of women have been battered, dominated, raped, tortured, and destroyed simply because they were women. These countless victims haunt the halls of history. Their presence unmasks the naivete of all our chauvinist efforts to deck those halls with heroic imagery.

My aim is not to exonerate nature. I am only calling attention to a rather important shift we are challenged to make in our understanding of an anguished world, suggesting that our century is witnessing what Metz calls "an anthropocentrism of suffering." We are less and less able to place utopian hopes in science and technology to save humanity from the terrors of nature, for those very tools have confronted us with far more dreadful horrors of history. The Enlightenment crusades against prejudice seem rather self-forgetful of the deeper strains of bias which have turned the Enlightenment tools of emancipation into new forms of slavery.[18]

### Agapic Praxis and Prophetic Theology

Acknowledging the manifold perversity of bias infecting all human, historical projects has at least two very important sets of consequences. The first set deals with closed options. Solidarity with the myriad victims of history cannot be genuine if it leads to either apathetic resignation or heroic recrimination. Such options are only illusory opposites, for both of them spring from the same oversight of bias responsible for our anguished world. Apathetic resignation trivializes the histories of suffering by muting their cry and claim on our consciences. Heroic recrimination seeks to distance itself from the histories of suffering by victimizing the victors, thereby making its own the very bias of the victors. These options are closed to the degree that we realize how they fail to get at the roots of bias and only in the long run add to the list of victims. The second set of consequences deals with the options open to those in genuine solidarity with the concrete histories of suffering. These options are many because the problem of bias is so diffuse in history. In this section I should like to concentrate upon the religious option, and then in the following sections indicate how that religious option relates to other options.

Apathetic resignation and heroic recrimination are closed options which cannot do justice to the massive dimensions of our anguished world with its myriad victims. These dimensions challenge us to participate in those communities of suffering which transcend the manifold biases of history through a compassionate refusal to be victims. Resignation and recrimination are human, all too human, responses to an anguished world. But, in being merely human responses, they end up dehumanizing those who choose them. The paradox of the human condition in an anguished world is that our profound desires to humanize and personalize ourselves and our world seem beyond the reach of our achievements. The victims of history are there, subversively to remind us that humankind on its own is quite literally a dead end. Stoic resignation might celebrate our status as cosmic orphans, but the celebration fizzles out too quickly, as Pascal observed, into the vast, cold emptiness of stellar space and time. Heroic recrimination enters valiantly into the struggles for emancipation and justice, only to face the prospect—so ominous in our nuclear age—that the warfare will end only in a pyrrhic victory when there are no more eyes or teeth left.[19]

The religious option is constituted in the confession that to struggle for the realization of justice in history, humankind is not simply on its own. In the presence of the untold victims of history, the religious option humbly acknowledges that we human beings cannot justify ourselves. Even the most utopian realization of justice in history would not "justify" the untold generations of dead victims.[20] There are many aspects of the religious option. I shall sketch only a few in terms of Christian religious options.

While the contemporary anthropocentrism of suffering challenges Christians in a new manner, an important element in the challenge is to realize how the realities to which it points are not new. Metz thematizes this in terms of memory. Some historians of religion maintain that a common element of all world religions is a transcending orientation to God as love immanent in human life.[21] This orientation was intensified in Christian discipleship: the transcendent God so loved us as to become incarnate in Jesus' life, death, and resurrection. In Christ God identifies with the victims of history. The polymorphous bias dehumanizing and depersonalizing human history is more than just human failure at self-actualization. It is sin, and at bottom sin against God-as-love incarnated in humankind. Christians—especially Roman Catholics—have tended for a variety of cultural reasons to understand revelation as the disclosure of truths otherwise unattainable by human reason.[22] The anthropocentrism of suffering is calling our attention to a more profound understanding of revelation. The narratives of the Old and New Testaments are not only a series of revelations of supernatural truths but also narratives inviting us to follow transformatively a revelation of values. In the teachings of Jesus, and in his life, death, and resurrection whereby the proclaimer became the proclaimed, the values of self-transcending love are revealed in a way reason alone could not deduce. The Kantian concern to interpret these values as eminently secularist values was met, not only by Hegel's recognition that secular reason discloses in history a "butcher's block," but also by Marx's analysis of the Kantian concern as provincially bourgeois, and by Kierkegaard's existential reflections on the fear and trembling, the sickness unto death, hounding human history.[23]

Agapic praxis is one way of summarizing what Bonhoeffer analyzed as *The Cost of Discipleship*, when he wrote: "There remains an experience of incomparable value. We have for once learnt to see the great events of world history from below, from the perspective of the outcast, the suspect, the maltreated, the powerless, the oppressed, the reviled."[24] The Christo-pathy of death and resurrection calls us to a cosuffering with the victims in their struggles to transcend victimhood and reveals a transformation of values which brings grace out of sin, life out of death, wisdom out of folly. Far from a passive resignation in the face of injustice, such a self-transcending love (*agape*) intensifies participation in the humanizing and personalizing historical efforts for justice.[25] For the praxis of agapic love, the following of Christ as revelatory of God as love, breaks the hold of bias on the human mind and heart. Faith, as a knowledge born of love, is not irrational. What is profoundly irrational is the continued heroic efforts of humankind to make it on its own in the face of dis-

torted, biased world history. From the perspective of the victims, religious faith is indeed a leap, but not a leap beyond reason. Rather, it is a leap away from the irrationality of sin and
bias into reason.[26] Just as self-transcending love transformatively
intensifies the quest for justice, so a faith born of that love transformatively intensifies reason into a wisdom. Such wisdom instinctively reacts against the biased irrationality which heroically parades as reason in the so-called calculations of the
nuclear arms race. Such wisdom cannot accept the biased distortions of an "instrumental rationality" which makes its compromises with things the way they are, and is concerned only
with doing those things more efficiently.[27] For the way things
are is continuing to victimize millions of human beings. If faith is
a leap from bias into a transforming reason still to be realized in
history, then hope is a leap from despair into a joy and trust that
even though we die trying, yet we shall live. As faith is a knowledge born of love, so hope is a desire and an imminent expectation born of love.[28]

From the first disciples down to our own day, communities of
Christians have lived this agapic praxis. Against all odds they
paid the cost of discipleship and the price of orthodoxy expressing this orthopraxis. They prophetically denounced by their
lives the biased distortions of a Christendom which tried again
and again (and still tries) to twist Christ into a symbol for humankind's heroic projects. Prophecy in Israel and in Christianity
recognizes that the religious option is never pure. Only God is
without bias or sin.[29] Conversion is always a withdrawal from
bias and sin; it is always a continuing transformation "not yet"
fully achieved. Religious solidarity with the victims of history is
never an easy, comfortable, automatic or cheap grace. Conversion can shatter; religious symbols and language can become the
property of a clerical elite who pay only lip service to the revelation of values. Religious authorities can too easily fall into patterns of domination and control. When this occurs in the religious option, sacralism emerges. Sacralism guarantees salvation
for the cheap price of a lip service orthodoxy and a routine obedience to law. God becomes identified with the mighty and powerful of this anguished world. Divine omnipotence becomes ter

rifying and threatening. Priests will protect—but for a price. The history of Israel played out this drama within a people. Israel was born as a protest against the sacralism of surrounding cultures and religions. But vocations, like birthrights, can easily be compromised. The struggle between monarchy and the prophets was later intensified to the point of apocalyptic expectation: from Davidic kingship to the kingship of Yahweh.[30] Jesus both inherited and transformed this ongoing critique of sacralism. Jesus' preaching and life-praxis tensively broke the sacralist tendency to identify the Kingdom of God with worldly power or might, with sacralist authoritarianism or the perspective of the victors in history. The good news is a prolonged passion narrative. Because Jesus' life-praxis and passion incarnated the identification of God with victimhood, it is no wonder that the parabler and proclaimer became the parable and proclaimed.[31] Discipleship demanded both a transvaluation of sacralist values and apocalyptic expectation. Transvaluation reversed the heroic expectations of identifying divine power with domination and oppression: divine power is revealed in weakness, in a kenotic love by the All Powerful emptying out into humanity. Apocalyptic expectation revealed a structure of time and history "from below," from the perspective of the victims of history. For the imminent expectation—the "Surely I am coming soon. Amen. Come, Lord Jesus!" closing the New Testament—of apocalyptic reveals the disjunctive temporality of victims expecting salvation which interrupts the continuity of physical time.[32] Prophetic narrative as intensified in apocalyptic expressed the agapic praxis revelatory of divine love identified with the weak, powerless, outcast, victim. As the Gospel of Matthew (chapter 25) indicates, this will be the criterion of judgment when the Son of Man comes.[33]

The anthropocentrism of suffering, as it deepens our understanding of Scripture, deepens our understanding of the struggles in the history of Christianity. There is always a tension between a bias toward sacralism and the communities of disciples whose agapic praxis and prophetic preaching cut against the grain of dominative world history. The sacralist bias is manifested in the continual temptation to identify the reign of God with Christian churches, to clothe Christ in the trappings of the mighty and powerful victors, heroes, or superstars of world history. Yet far less ostentatious and pretentious, there were also the "little ones," the small, transformative communities disrupting the worldly predictability of sacralist bias by their agapic praxis and prophetic-apocalyptic expectations. It is no different in our day. Where do we discern the Spirit of Christ? The Vatican curia or Catholic Worker communities? The World Council of Churches or Taize? The Christian Broadcasting Network or Sojourner communities? CELAM or the *comunidades de base*? The very juxtaposition of these contrasts indicates the *tensive* quality of agapic praxis and prophetically narrative theologies. The sociological dualisms of institution versus charisma, of church versus sect do not adequately articulate the tensive dialectics in this following of Christ.[34]

Such dualisms are ways of rationalizing the tensive character by viewing it from the perspective of dominative world history with its biases. It allows those in power to treat the transformative communities as marginal, as anomalous, as peripheral. It is a more modern form of a very old biased flight from understanding and conversion: the kings tried it with the prophets, Pilate and the priests tried it with Jesus; the Roman Imperium with the early Christians; Holy Roman emperors and Vatican authorities with reform movements . . . The list goes on. What it tells us is the importance of transformative communities challenging the sacralist biases by a continual and ongoing dedication to agapic praxis and prophetic-apocalyptic expectation as the heart of Christian discipleship. Such communities, in challenging the apathetic resignation within themselves and the churches, must struggle not to become embittered and to deform their witness into a heroic recrimination which would lead them to lose the *tensive* dialectic of discipleship by repudiating their oneness with the many victims of history. One form of such a repudiation, to be especially guarded against, would be to yield to the sacralist bias by repudiating the churches, thereby allowing the dominative authorities to continue in their biased flight from understanding and abandoning the victims with their imminent expectation.[35]

## Noetic Praxis and Political Theology

An agapic praxis of ongoing conversion, as a continual withdrawal from social sin as bias, and prophetic-apocalyptic narratives expressive of a disjunctive imminent expectation of redemption by the victims of history—these are the foundations of all Christian theologies committed to be hearers and doers of the Word. They are constants providing the undertow, throughout the past two thousand years, going against the currents of dominative world history. It is difficult to make generalizations since agapic praxis and prophetic-apocalyptic narratives have taken on many distinct and different forms depending upon the situations. This recurrent undertow, however, is the continuous struggle of those adopting the Christian religious option in our anguished world. They incarnate the transforming values of faith, hope, and love by which human history will be judged and redeemed. The undertow might be described as the foundational level of religious praxis in and throughout history.

The recent developments in political theologies might be described as reflective efforts to mediate the transformative values of such religious praxis to other intellectual, moral, and social options. The religious option is not the only way of responding to an anguished world. This is especially true in our contemporary situation marked as it is by a dialectic of Enlightenment. The social sins spawning so much anguish and suffering for millions and millions of human beings are, as the first section indicated, not all caused by sacralist bias. Indeed, it would be a concession to sacralism to imagine that religious options alone could remedy or heal the manifold histories of suffering. Theology cannot only rest upon the religious foundations of agapic praxis; nor can theology exhaust its mission in prophetic and apocalyptic narrative modes of expression. Whenever theology tries to go on its own way it becomes eventually distorted into a sacralist fideism, or fundamentalism. Agapic praxis itself is a conversion—a *metanoia* which literally means a "change of mind (*nous*)"—whereby the revelation of God's identification with victims begins to heal the irrationalities of the manifold biases which harden human hearts and darken human reason. The leap of faith, as a knowledge born of love, is a leap into sapiential reason, away from the irrationalities which anguish nature and history. Prophetic-apocalyptic narrative expressions of agapic praxis, whether in liturgies, spiritual discernment, poetry, art, or music, reach deeply and transformatively into the pathos of the human psyche and spirit. The wisdom nurtured there, the revelation of transcendently immanent values, gives impetus to a questioning which must find expression in a reflective intellectual or noetic praxis.[36] Theology is a reflective noetic praxis which mediates the transformative values and narratives of religion to cultures and societies.[37]

How massive this task is today can be inferred from the manifold effects of bias sketched above. Theologies and theologians certainly are not immune from biases. Noetic praxis, similar to agapic praxis, is always a painful withdrawal from bias. This is especially so in theology, since, being constituted by both faith and reason, theology is open to infection, not only by the biases distorting the religious options but also by those distorting all the other options (intellectual, moral, social) as well. One can find theologies ideologically supporting almost every bias that ever raised its ugly head in history. No wonder that Catherine of Siena and Dorothy Day often prayed for "the poor theologians." Theologies have abounded attempting to rationalize imperialism, colonialism, racism, sexism, capitalism, militarism, totalitarianism, communism, sacralism, atheistic secularism, consumerism, multinationalism, fascism, anti-Semitism, Nazism, chauvinism, technocratic elitism, clerical authoritarianism, etc. It is difficult to think that theology was ever considered more than a dumping ground of biases. Theologians have always been found who will readily join in the parade of the latest social or cultural, ecclesial or political, heroic victor whose drums drown out the cries of the victims. Dante depicts the torments in hell and purgatory for such theological malpractice. Why purgatory? Because very often theologians are just doing the best they can; they tag along a little breathless and a little late in the hope of showing the relevance of the parade (*Zeitgeist*) to the gospel message or vice versa, unaware of the juggernaut further down the road. They are trying not to bury their talents.[38]

The contemporary anthropocentric turn to the victims of history has profound and far-reaching implications for theology. As Lonergan observes, the age of innocent theory is past. Even if theory never was innocent, at least now we should know how biased theory can be. Noetic praxis as intellectual conversion can no longer be taken for granted. It must be thematized explicitly in an anthropocentric turn to the questioning human subject whereby we appropriate our own cognitive desires and expectations with their related and recurrent operations.[39] For the notion of a "pure reason" in history is an illusion with which we can no longer live. Reason is always ongoing, not only in the sense that every answer always raises further questions but also in the sense that reason is never fully realized in history. Human, historical reason is always practical, always a withdrawal from biased beliefs, as reason is yet to be realized in society and history.[40] We can no longer live with the illusion of pure reason because of its manifold victims. The dialectic of the Enlightenment provides a sad commentary on this. The Enlightenment promised human emancipation through reason. But it naively trusted in a pure reason embodied (supposedly) in mathematical hard-headedness and natural scientific technology. Such a pure reason not only created ever more wondrous machines but also became increasingly assimilated to its own mechanistic creations.

The "success" of mathematics and natural sciences meant their methods became the canon of all exact knowledge for the human sciences—what could not be quantified somehow lacked meaning. The "success" of technology meant that the machine became the model of rational order—what could not be programmed somehow should not exist. Human sciences began to treat humanity as made in the image of its own mechanized products. Organic and psychic processes were no more than highly complex physical-mechanical events. Mind and consciousness were dismissed as illusory, sooner rather than later to be mapped out in cybernetic, bio-computer input-output schemata. Work was "Taylorized" into mechanistically regulated assembly line productivity. Interpersonal relations became techniques of successful role playing. Community values took a back seat to the demands of mobility with urbanization and industrialization. Nature became a reservoir and junk yard for the expanding megamachine. In short, pure reason became in practice an instrumental rationality cleverly devising more clean and efficient techniques to put at the service of a radically biased conduct (praxis).[41]

The noetic praxis of theorizing cannot be taken for granted, for as Metz correctly observes:

> the world of our experience is in fact a secondary or meta-world, in other words, a world which, in itself and in its deepest reality, bears the deep impression of many systems and theories, and which can therefore only be experienced and possibly changed in and through these systems and theories. If this fact is forgotten, the result may easily be the acceptance of an uncritical notion of praxis. A praxis which fails to take into account the complex structure of the world or our experience of it as secondary will therefore inevitably remain sporadic and ineffective.[42]

An illustration of this is the comment of a very dedicated member of a Catholic Worker community who recently remarked how important intellectual analysis of the systemic injustices is in order to promote more effectively critical action. Without such analysis social action would be like "putting bandaids on a leper." The problem of the Enlightenment is dialectical, that is, the intellectual options it has developed are not all biased. As Christians cannot believe that evil is coequal with God, so we cannot claim that any position is totally and irrevocably biased. Noetic praxis commits us to the task of dialectically discerning the values and disvalues, carefully removing (in Lonergan's words) the cancer of the biased "flight from understanding without destroying the organs of intelligence." Political theology realizes this imperative in Metz's long and taxing efforts to establish a Graduate Theological Research Center at the University of Bielefeld in which theology would participate critically in the many interdisciplinary research projects of the university, as well as initiate interdisciplinary research projects of its own between theology and all the other sciences and disciplines.[43] Such a noetic praxis of theologizing would develop academically institutionalized ways of promoting an intellectual conversion (*metanoia*) whereby the suffering witness of the victims of history would transformatively challenge the systems and theories constitutive of our world experience.

The anthropocentric turn to these victims means that all theologies are challenged to engage in such a noetic praxis of critical self-reflection. In this sense, political theology is a foundational effort inasmuch as it articulates criteria immanent in both faith and reason for dialectically discerning intellectual options conducive to, or biasedly destructive of, faith as a knowledge born of agapic love and reason as yet to be realized in society and history. It is also reconstructive inasmuch as its foundational criteria lead to a reconstruction of Christian traditions from the perspective of the victims of history.[44] It develops both a hermeneutics of recovery regarding the transcending values incarnated in overcoming the many histories of suffering, and a hermeneutics of suspicion regarding the dehumanizing disvalues alienating and distorting history.

Universities and academic pursuits are in need of such an intellectual apostolate. They have contributed in no small measure to the alienation and victimization of human life on this planet. The noetic praxis of political theology would join with others in attacking this sorry performance at its roots: namely, how intelligence has been biased by a knowledge born of fear. The heroic projects of a "humankind on its own" are the bitter fruits of knowledge born of fear—and many realize how alienating academic life is as it socializes generations of students into fearful and heroic competition to determine who is fit to survive. Too often universities turn out heroic elites who will use that fear-engendered knowledge in order to oppress and manipulate both nature and their fellow human beings. Religious faith, as a knowledge born of love, is a constitutive element of truly practical reason, that is, reason committed to expanding the effective freedom of all human beings in history. The early emergence of universities in the West from the monastic and cathedral schools contains many subversive memories which we need to recall.[45]

One such memory recalls the dangers of sacralism and how reactions against it have led many to adopt inadequate moral options in their efforts to liberate humankind. Not only was the Abelard affair symptomatic of the undifferentiated sacralism of the Middle Ages, it was tragically prophetic. The sacralist bias led to a deadly identification—remember the crusades, the wars of religion—of the Kingdom of God with a religio-political hierarchical authoritarianism in the later Middle Ages. From the Renaissance onward criticisms of this sacralist religiosity increased and indicated how it distorted human life and repressed the moral imperatives of effective human freedom. In the seventeenth century these morally inspired criticisms led to a defensive, clerical sacralism (especially in Roman Catholicism) which tended to spread the mantle of religion over the opinions or whims of biasedly ignorant *men*. This defensive sacralism provoked, from the nineteenth century onward, an equally undifferentiated and offensive secularism. The well-intentioned moral aspirations of this secularism are well documented in Ernest Becker's *The Structure of Evil*.[46] Yet the effect was an alienating transition—as Max Weber intimated—from a hierarchic sacralist authoritarianism to a bureaucratic secularist authoritarianism. Like all authoritarianisms, the two tend to reinforce each other over the heads of peoples and communities. The illusion of a god identical with ecclesial-social institutions is not radically different from the illusion of a humankind identical with political-economic institutions.

Sacralism and secularism turn out to be illusory opposites, the bias of one reinforcing that of the other. Humankind ends up the loser, suffering under the yokes of ecclesial and bureaucratic elites. Political interaction is reduced to the futile efforts on the part of crisis management to control and balance competing pressure groups. Rather than nurturing truly open and public discussions of values informing policy, politics is absorbed into amoral forms of social engineering governed by the dictates of an instrumental irrationality—the one-dimensionality against which Marcuse warned.[47] Restoring the moral options to political life will, in part, entail an elaboration of what Metz spells out as the dialectic of redemption and political emancipation. The secularist success story of replacing *Deus Salvator* with *Homo Emancipator* in our times takes on very different colors when viewed from the eyes of the victims. Since God was no longer around to blame for the concrete histories of suffering, political orientations became infected with biased defense mechanisms to exonerate us from responsibility for suffering.[48]

Conservatives try to atrophy past victories by immunizing the status quo against its critics through legal, economic, humanitarian, and armed force. Liberals make nature the scapegoat for suffering: human failures are ascribed to an unenlightened past which will be absolved by the advance of science and technology. Marxists have no difficulty in attributing the histories of suffering to those enemies of the proletariat who still wield power in history and so impede the inevitable success of the march toward a party-planned utopia. Such defense mechanisms find their apotheosis in those advocates of technocracy who deny human freedom and dignity. Just as some Enlightenment theodicies found the final solution to the problems of God's existence in the face of human suffering by denying that God exists, so a contemporary "anthropodicy" faced with human suffering proclaims that humanity does not exist. Only matter in motion exists. The political can only be known by quantifying statistics.[49] The moral option itself either disappears from public political discourse or finds such biased statistical expressions in movements like the Moral Majority. Clearly, this dialectic of redemption and emancipation does not suggest that no moral options exist for contemporary political discourse. Quite the contrary, as with the intellectual options, so the moral options springing from the Enlightenment are not all biased. Human and civil rights with all they imply for democracy and freedom are a legacy subversive of biased defense mechanisms. The aim of the dialectical discernment is not to deny but to strengthen that legacy by calling attention to how differently that legacy is received on the part of the victims of history for whom the very right to live is continually threatened.[50]

Finally, the noetic praxis of political theology dialectically criticizes the social options globally confronting humankind today. Those options tend to be narrowly "Atlantic" in the sense that late capitalism and state socialism have tried heroically to impose their ideologies—which are European and North American in origin—on the social and economic processes of the entire globe. This biased provincialism of the so-called superpowers— whether governmental or transnational superpowers—has made it increasingly difficult for peoples in Africa, Latin America, and Asia to develop their own indigenous social options. This new form of colonialism, like previous forms of colonialism, is too often supported by ecclesial authorities whose sacralist bias matches the secularist bias of governmental or economic super- powers. Pope John Paul II's recent encyclical *On Human Work* decisively criticized this secularist bias and committed Catholi- cism to promoting alternatives to late capitalism and to state so- cialism. A noetic praxis attentive to the values of faith as a knowledge born of love and to the prophetic-apocalyptic narra- tives of the victims of history must also collaborate with all those groups in Third World countries seeking to break the heroic hold of late capitalism and state socialism on the social options of their countries.

One extremely important aspect of such collaboration—an as- pect Hegel and Marx initiated with the dialectic of master and slave—is to realize how solidarity with the victims in the mod- ern economic colonies makes us attentive to the many victims in our own neighborhoods.[51] As I mentioned before, welfarism is colonialism *ad intra.* The sufferings caused by late capitalism and state socialism the world over only indicate how profoundly ignorant and shortsighted the competitive macroeconomic sys- tems are. Contemporary Christian social teachings have contin- ually criticized the alienating shortcomings of both late capital- ism and state socialism. But, as liberation theologians rightly point out, if these criticisms—however justified in themselves— are not to degenerate into value-neutral legitimizations of the status quo, then we face the immense task of articulating critical social and economic theories and practices capable of con- cretely and dialectically overcoming the alienations so massively present in both. Moralistic appeals to the common good, subsi- diarity, and the just wage are hardly sufficient. Nor are rhetori- cal flourishes about class warfare when, as John McMurtry and many others indicate, the capitalist classes are concretely re- placed in state socialisms with party bureaucratic classes.[52] A

noetic praxis engaged in the anthropocentric turn to the victims
of history cannot succumb to an instrumentalization of dialectical criticism—which would be its death—by maintaining that
*the only* social options are either late capitalism or state socialism. That would only legitimate the present global status quo
and betray the creative criticism of Marx's own praxis of
theorizing, not to mention the betrayal of millions of victims.
The proletariat deserves infinitely more than a parade in celebration of superpower socialism. A dialectical retrieval of Marx
by political theology demands nothing less than a commitment
to collaborate in articulating a new macroeconomic knowledge
of the production process attentive to the values incarnate in
agapic praxis and prophetic-apocalyptic narratives. The victims
of our anguished world deserve no less.[53]

### North American Tasks

In conclusion, the noetic praxis of political theology in North
America will involve an extensive collaboration within contexts
characterized by a global perspective. A global perspective is
intrinsic to political theology in the United States insofar as economic and political life in the United States is itself intrinsically
global in its effects and consequences. There is also a theological
reason for such a perspective: the concrete histories of suffering are simultaneously immanent in particular places and times
and by that very immanence transcend those particularities
to become one with all victims throughout space and time.
Doing political theology within a global context would involve,
among many other elements I cannot list here, the following
tasks:

1. Collaboration with critical sociologists and critical psychologists to explore the roots of biases feeding the militarism, racism, sexism, mutinational colonialism, sacralism, and secularist consumerism alienating social life in North America;
2. Collaboration with critical economists to develop the elements of a systemic macroeconomic analysis which would aim
   at a critique of late capitalisms and state socialisms as they are
   now dysfunctioning globally. In North America this especially
   means offering a critical support and collaboration with the

small but intelligent groups of economists who take Marx seriously;

3. Collaboration with critical environmentalists and ecotechnologists to develop alternatives to the megamechanistic destruction of the ecology and the shortsighted quest for industrial exponential growth;

4. Collaboration with critical political scientists to unmask, and begin to envisage alternatives to, the alienating depoliticization so rampant in North American life due to the so-called politics as social engineering;

5. Collaboration with critical historians to aid in the reconstruction of the many histories of suffering in North America, especially relative to the colonial exploitation of native Americans, slavery, the revolutionary and didactic phases of Enlightenment in America, the immigration periods, and the labor movements;

6. Collaboration with other theologians to expose the many biases alienating religious faith and practice in North America, especially in the many forms these take of institutionalized sacralism, and to discern and promote the many communities living out agapic praxis;

7. Collaboration with other critical colleagues in educational systems to support policies—especially in religiously affiliated schools—aimed at actually realizing education for justice with the poor and oppressed. The middle class only has two options: either to *transcend* "downwards" by casting its lot with the victims in the struggle to overcome injustice, or to be *forced* downwards by the malfunctioning of the macroeconomic process.

These and any other tasks for political theology in North America are not ends in themselves. Genuine noetic praxis is not meant to fill libraries with learned and critically social volumes to be consulted occasionally by colleagues or students in a history of ideas course. Genuine noetic praxis does not aim at creating another set of academic elites whose fear-engendered knowledge will equip them to manipulate and lead the masses. Genuine noetic praxis, especially as that should be operative in political theology, aims to transform human history, redeeming it through a knowledge born of a subject-empowering, life-giving love which heals the biases needlessly victimizing millions of our brothers and sisters. *Vox victimarum vox Dei.* The cries of the victims are the voice of God. To the extent that those cries are not heard above the din of our political, cultural, economic, social, and ecclesial celebrations or bickerings, we have already begun a descent into hell. "For I was hungry and you gave me no food. I was thirsty and you gave me no drink. I was a stranger and you did not welcome me, naked and you did not clothe me, sick and in prison and you did not visit me" (Mt. 24:42f.).

## NOTES

1. Cf. Ernest Becker, *The Structure of Evil* (New York: George Braziller, 1968) pp. 3–98; Floyd W. Matson, *The Broken Image* (New York: Doubleday, 1966), pp. 15–29, 66–110.

2. Ernest Becker, op. cit., pp. 135–249; Lewis Mumford, *The Condition of Man* (New York: Harcourt Brace Jovanovich, Inc., 1944), pp. 301–89.

3. Ernest Becker, *Escape From Evil* (New York: Macmillan, 1975); Floyd W. Matson, *The Idea of Man* (New York: Delta Books, 1976), pp. 1–109.

4. From letter of Marx to Engels, *Werke* (Berlin: 1959), vol. 30, p. 131. Marx was later to express hesitations about Darwin's work. Cf. David McLellan, *Karl Marx* (New York: Harper & Row, 1973), pp. 423ff.

5. Ernest Becker, *The Structure of Evil*, pp. 211–49; Floyd Matson, *The Idea of Man*, pp. 110–33, 196–210; Paul Roazen, *Freud and His Followers* (New York: Meridian, 1974), pp. 96–145; Daniel Yankelovich and William Barrett, *Ego and Instinct: The Psychoanalytic View of Human Nature—Revised* (New York: Random House, 1970); Paul Ricoeur, *Freud and Philosophy*, trans. D. Savage (New Haven: Yale University Press, 1970), pp. 69–86.

6. Cf. Gil Eliot, *Twentieth Century Book of the Dead* (New York: Scribner, 1972); cf. also chap. 2 below.

7. Georges Gusdorf, *De l'histoire des sciences a l'histoire de la pensée* (Paris: Payot, 1966), pp. 93–126. Gusdorf, *La révolution galiléenne* (Paris: Payot, 1969), pp. 17–122.

8. Bernard Lonergan, *Insight: A Study of Human Understanding* (New York: Philosophical Library, 1957), pp. 191–244; Paul Ricoeur,

*Freedom and Nature* (Northwestern University Press, 1966), pp. 20–34. Space prohibits a detailed analysis of the similarities and differences between Ricoeur's notion of the fault and Lonergan's notion of bias. For an insightful correlation of these notions with social sin, cf. Patrick Kerans, *Sinful Social Structures* (New York: Paulist Press, 1974).

9. Ivan Illich, *Medical Nemesis: The Expropriation of Health* (New York: Pantheon Books, 1976).

10. Susan George, *How the Other Half Dies: The Real Reasons for World Hunger* (Montclair, New Jersey: Allanheld, Osmun and Co., 1977); Frances Moore Lappé and Joseph Collins, *Food First: Beyond the Myth of Scarcity* (New York: Ballantine Books, 1977); Jack A. Nelson, *Hunger for Justice: The Politics of Food and Faith* (Maryknoll: Orbis, 1980).

11. Willy Brandt (Chairman), *North-South: A Program for Survival* (Cambridge: MIT Press, 1980); Mihajlo Mesarovic and Eduard Pestel, *Mankind at the Turning Point* (New York: E. P. Dutton and Co., 1974); Jan Tinbergen (ed.), *Reshaping the International Order* (New York: E. P. Dutton and Co., 1976); Ervin Laszlo et al., *Goals for Mankind* (New York: E. P. Dutton and Co., 1977); Gerald and Patricia Mische, *Toward a Human World Order* (New York: Paulist Press, 1977); M. Albert and R. Hahnel, *Socialism in Theory and Praxis*, 2 vols. (Boston: South End Press, 1981).

12. Joseph O'Malley and Keith Algozin (eds.), *Rubel on Karl Marx* (New York: Cambridge University Press, 1981), pp. 82–229.

13. Matthew Lamb, "The Production Process and Exponential Growth," in F. Lawrence (ed.) *Lonergan Workshop* (Missoula: Scholars Press, 1978), vol. 1.

14. Philip Green, *The Pursuit of Inequality* (New York: Pantheon Books, 1978).

15. Andre Gorz, *Ecology as Politics* (Boston: South End Press, 1980); Carolyn Merchant, *The Death of Nature* (San Francisco: Harper & Row, 1980).

16. Naomi R. Goldenberg, "Jung After Feminism," in Rita Gross (ed.), *Beyond Androcentrism* (Missoula: Scholars Press, 1977), pp. 53–66; June Singer, *Androgyny: Toward a New Theory of Sexuality* (Garden City, New York: Anchor Press, 1976).

17. Mary Daly, *Gyn/Ecology: The Metaethics of Radical Feminism* (Boston: Beacon Press, 1978); Carol P. Christ, *Diving Deep and Surfacing: Women Writers on Spiritual Quest* (Boston: Beacon Press, 1980).

18. Max Horkheimer and Theodor W. Adorno, *Dialectic of Enlightenment*, trans. John Cumming (New York: Herder and Herder, 1972); Paul Connerton, *The Tragedy of Enlightenment* (New York: Cambridge University Press, 1980).

19. Cf. M. Lamb, "A Response to Bernard Lonergan," in *Catholic Theological Society of American Proceedings* 32 (1977): 22–30; J. B. Metz, *Faith in History and Society* (New York: Seabury Press, 1980), pp. 100–35.

20. Helmut Peukert, *Wissenschaftstheorie-Handlungstheorie-Fundamentale Theologie* (Frankfurt: Suhrkamp, 1978), pp. 317–55.

21. F. Heiler, "The History of Religions as a Preparation for the Cooperation of Religions," *The History of Religions,* ed. M. Eliade and J. Kitagawa (Chicago: Chicago University Press, 1959), pp. 142–53; B. Lonergan, *Method in Theology* (New York: Herder and Herder, 1972), pp. 101–20; M. Lamb, *History, Method and Theology* (Missoula: Scholars Press, 1978), pp. 497–506; Friedrich Heiler (ed.), *Die Religionen der Menscheit* (Stuttgart: Philipp Reclam, 1962).

22. Quentin Quesnell, "Beliefs and Authenticity," in *Creativity and Method,* ed. M. Lamb (Milwaukee: Marquette University Press, 1980), pp. 173–83.

23. David Tracy, *The Analogical Imagination: Christian Theology and the Culture of Pluralism* (New York: Crossroad, 1981), pp. 339–70.

24. Dietrich Bonhoeffer, *Letters and Papers From Prison* (London: Collins, 1971), p. 17.

25. Rosemary Haughton, *The Catholic Thing* (Springfield, Illinois: Templegate Publishers, 1979), pp. 131–202; idem, *The Passionate God* (New York: Paulist Press, 1981), pp. 129–73, 279–322.

26. Lonergan, "Lectures on the Philosophy of Education," (Cincinnati: Xavier University, 1959, n.p.), lecture 3, pp. 10–13; W. Loewe, "Dialectics of Sin: Lonergan's Insight and the Critical Theory of Max Horkheimer," in *Anglican Theological Review* 41/2 (1979):224–45.

27. Max Horkheimer, *Critique of Instrumental Reason* (New York: Seabury Press, 1974), pp. 1–61, 136–58; also W. Loewe as cited in n. 26 above.

28. M. Douglas Meeks, *Origins of the Theology of Hope* (Philadelphia: Fortress Press, 1974); Lonergan, *Method,* pp. 101–12, 285–94.

29. Gerhard von Rad, *The Message of the Prophets* (New York: Harper & Row, 1962), pp. 15–99. For a thorough study of the social critical import of early Israel, cf. Norman K. Gottwald, *The Tribes of Yahweh* (Maryknoll, New York: Orbis Books, 1979).

30. Sean McEvenue, "The Rise of David Story and the Search for a Story to Live By," in *Creativity and Method,* ed. M. Lamb, pp. 185–95 and references given there. For a study of how the Old Testament has contributed to the desire for social change in Western civilization, cf. the literary study by Herbert N. Schneidau, *Sacred Discontent* (Berkeley: University of California Press, 1977).

31. Ernst Käsemann, *Jesus Means Freedom* (Philadelphia: Fortress Press, 1977); Norman Perrin, *Jesus and the Language of the Kingdom* (Philadelphia: Fortress Press, 1976); David Tracy, *Blessed Rage for*

*Order* (New York: Seabury Press, 1975), pp. 120–45; Ben F. Meyer, *The Aims of Jesus* (London SCM Press, 1979), pp. 129–73.

32. On the corrective which apocalyptic offers to eschatology, cf. Metz, *Faith in History and Society*, pp. 3–13, 169–79.

33. Cf. Dorothy Soelle, *The Truth Is Concrete* (New York: Herder and Herder, 1969); J. B. Metz, *Followers of Christ* (New York: Burns and Oates/Paulist Press, 1978).

34. J. B. Metz, *The Emergent Church* (New York: Crossroad, 1981), pp. 48–94. Metz clearly indicates how basic Christian communities should be understood in dialectical continuity with the larger institutional structures of the churches.

35. Sergio Torres and John Eagleson (eds.), *The Challenge of Basic Christian Communities* (Maryknoll, New York: Orbis Books, 1981).

36. Concerning the nature and characteristics of intellectual or noetic praxis, cf. chaps. 2 and 3 of this book.

37. Cf. Lonergan, *Method,* pp. xi and xiiff.

38. M. Lamb, *History, Method and Theology,* pp. 4–19 and references given there.

39. Ibid., pp. 357–529.

40. Cf. chap. 2 and the references given in n. 18 above. Lonergan's notion of the pure and unrestricted desire to know is radically different from Kant's notion of pure reason. Lonergan's notion is precisely the imperative to raise ever further questions which grounds the self-correcting processes of learning and doing. It is also, therefore, the ground for the praxis of ongoing intellectual conversion whereby bias is overcome. For the contrast of this with Kant's notion, see Giovanni Sala, *Das Apriori in der menschlichen Erkenntnis: Eine Studie über Kants Kritik der reinen Vernunft und Lonergans Insight* (Meisenheim: Verlag Anton Hain, 1971), pp. 237–82.

41. Metz, *Faith in History and Society*, pp. 14–48, 100–35.

42. Ibid., pp. 4–5.

43. Lonergan, *Insight*, p. xiv. For a preliminary account of Metz's Bielefeld project, cf. J. B. Metz and T. Rendtorff (eds.), *Die Theologie in der Interdisziplinären Forschung* (Düsseldorf: Bertelsmann, 1971). At this writing it appears that this new way of doing theology will not be institutionalized at Bielefeld due to ecclesiastical procrastination in giving the needed authorization. This project has consumed much of Professor Metz's time and energy over the past decade and clearly indicates how his concern with apocalyptic is not Barthian but has sought instead a very practical mediation to the sciences and scholarly disciplines.

44. Francis Fiorenza, "Political Theology as Foundational Theology," in *Catholic Theological Society of America Proceedings* 32 (1977): 142–77.

45. Lynn White, *Medieval Religion and Technology* (Berkeley: University of California Press, 1978), pp. 329–38; Hasting Rashdall, *The*

*Universities of Europe in the Middle Ages*, 2 ed., ed. F. M. Powicke and A. B. Emden (Oxford University Press, 1936), vol. 1; J. Leclerq, *The Love of Learning and the Desire for God* (London: Darton, Longman and Todd, 1970).

46. Ernest Becker, *The Structure of Evil*, pp. 307–82; Hans Blumenberg, *Die Legitimität der Neuzeit* (Frankfurt: Suhrkamp, 1966); Robert M. Wallace, "Progress, Secularization and Modernity: The Löwith-Blumenberg Debate," in *New German Critique*, no. 22 (Winter 1981): 63–79.

47. Herbert Marcuse, *One Dimensional Man* (Boston: Beacon Press, 1968).

48. Ernest Becker, *The Denial of Death* (New York: The Free Press, 1973); Becker, *Beyond Alienation* (New York: George Braziller, 1969), pp. 165–225.

49. Politics has become devaluated in modern times; it is no longer primarily a quest of communities for consensus but rather a manipulating activity of elites attempting to engineer policies decided upon by the elites themselves. Cf. Jürgen Habermas, *Legitimation Crisis* (Boston: Beacon Press, 1975), pp. 1–32, 95–143; Thomas McCarthy, *The Critical Theory of Jürgen Habermas* (Cambridge: MIT Press, 1979), pp. 1–39, 358–86.

50. It was Marx who first called attention to the difference between political rights and human rights in a systematic way. Cf. Joseph O'Malley (ed.), *Karl Marx: Critique of Hegel's "Philosophy of Right"* (London: Cambridge University Press, 1970), pp. 5–142.

51. For an analysis of how exploitation affects neighborhood communities and how community organizing can counteract such exploitation, cf. Harry C. Boyte, *The Backyard Revolution* (Philadelphia: Temple University Press, 1980).

52. John McMurtry, *The Structure of Marx's World-View* (Princeton University Press, 1978), pp. 72–187; Rudolf Bahro, *The Alternative in Eastern Europe* (London: Verso, 1981). On Bahro's concern for the religious dimensions of community building, cf. his dialogue with Johann B. Metz, "Der Geist und die Basis," in *Publik Forum*, no. 11 (29 May 1981): 15–19.

53. There is need to develop a critical macroeconomic analysis which would unmask the alienations operative in both late capitalism and state socialism. This task demands an attention to the actually existing macroeconomic phases of surplus expansion and distribution. In my opinion the as yet unpublished macroeconomic manuscripts of Bernard Lonergan provide some of the more important categories for such a critical analysis. Cf. Michael Gibbons, "Insight and Emergence: An Introduction to Lonergan's Circulation Analysis," in M. Lamb (ed.), *Creativity and Method*, pp. 529–41, for a very brief discussion of these as yet unpublished manuscripts.

# Chapter 2

# Critical Theory and the End of Intellectual Innocence

If the events of the twentieth century illustrate anything, the fallacy of "pure" reason or "pure" theory would be near the top of the list. Theory and reason as concretely embodied in scientific and technological research have continued to draw very heavily upon those reservoirs of fear and aggression more commonly called defense budgets. Not only in the nuclear arms race but in almost every sphere of modern, industrialized life, science and scholarship have been too ready too often to legitimate and to strengthen the dominative interests of the highest bidders. The innocent faith of the Enlightenment in pure reason has crumbled under the devastation of two world wars, the holocaust, nuclear arms races, environmental pollution, iatrogenic disease, and dwindling confidence in democracy on the part of both capitalist and socialist "experts." In such a mental climate it is not surprising that many North American intellectuals have turned to the representatives of the Frankfurt School of Social Research and the critical theory they pioneered.[1] Journals have multiplied devoted to publishing both translations of European critical theory and essays articulating critical categories which analyze the dialectics of decline in America.[2] The last decade witnessed a series of serious studies by Americans on the critical theory of the Frankfurt School, as well as on the many varieties of Marxist critical theory generally—not to mention a veritable spate of translations.[3]

Similar to its European counterparts, American critical theory involves correlations between critical Marxist positions and a whole series of other philosophical and social scientific perspectives (e.g., existentialism, phenomenology, hermeneutics, structuralism, semiotics, functionalism, symbolic interactionism, social psychological developmentalism, ontologism, etc.). Critical theory is a fundamental methodological enterprise not only concerned with sociology and philosophy but also with such diverse fields as epistemology, psychology, literary criticism, economics, aesthetics, education, anthropology, political science, and theology.[4] Although the debates among American critical theorists are often more intense than their exchanges with opponents, I do believe that certain common characteristics of critical theory can be delineated. The challenge *of* critical theory is to face squarely the radical critique of society provided by Marxist perspectives. The challenge *to* critical theory is to elaborate an understanding of praxis capable of genuinely transforming contemporary social relationships. Both of these challenges are, in varying ways, common to most work in critical theory.

In what follows I shall sketch some of the main elements involved in each of these challenges relative to sociology and human destiny. While I depend heavily upon the more classical writings of the Frankfurt School of critical theory, e.g., upon those of Max Horkheimer, Theodor Adorno, Walter Benjamin, and Herbert Marcuse, I shall also attempt to indicate American contributions and criticisms. Although North American scholars have till now tended more to interpret European critical theory rather than significantly change it, there are signs of very creative changes in the making.[5]

## The Challenge of Critical Theory

The challenge of critical theory consists in its varied efforts to reassert the critical potential of Marx's social analysis vis-à-vis both the positivist prejudices of sociology in late capitalism and the authoritarian idealist prejudices in state-socialist or communist sociology. This challenge of critical theory marks at least the beginning of the end of innocent critique. Where some suspect that this challenge undermines Marxism, the proponents of critical theory—correctly, in my judgment—view their challenge as important correctives to a Marxist dogmatism unfaithful to essential elements of Marx's own dialectical critique. Those elements involve insights into the dialectical functioning of social relationships in their concrete totality and particularity.

The challenge of critical theory is to end innocent critique. By innocent criticism I mean that type of critical perspective so central in the development of modern culture: criticism unaware of its own presuppositions and thereby tending to erect itself as *the* criterion of all criticism. Modernity understood itself as a critical and rational break with the past, as ushering in a new order of things—*novus ordo saeclorum* as the coined phrase has it, or the *rerum novarum* seriously pondered by Leo XIII. Against any superficial self-understanding of modernity the writings of Walter Benjamin, Theodor Adorno, and Max Horkheimer pose the stumbling block of contradiction: "Only he who recognizes the most modern as the ever-identical serves that which would be different."[6] Modernity is, underneath its gleaming facade of technological expertise, really archaic. In their *The Dialectic of Enlightenment* Adorno and Horkheimer develop the antithetical or "inverse" insights into how scientific reason is mythic, how enlightened liberal morality is barbaric, how technological progress is retrogression.[7] Benjamin caught this inverse insight imaginally:

> Marx says, revolutions are the locomotives of world history. But perhaps it is really totally different. Perhaps revolutions are the grasp by the human race travelling in this train for the emergency brake.[8]

And, in a thesis which captured the negativity of theology and Marxism, Benjamin wrote:

> There is a picture by Klee called "Angelus Novus." An angel is presented in it who looks as if he were about to move away from something at which he is staring. His eyes are wide open, his mouth is agape, his wings are spread. The angel of history must look like that. His face is turned toward the past. Where a chain of events appears to *us*, *he* sees one single catastrophe which relentlessly piles wreckage upon wreckage, and hurls them before his feet. The angel would like to stay, awaken the dead and make whole that which has been smashed. But a storm is blowing from Paradise; it has gotten caught in his wings, and it is so strong that the angel can no longer

close them. The storm drives him irresistibly into the future to which his back is turned, while the pile of debris
before him grows toward the sky. That which we name
progress is *this* storm.[9]

If, as Benjamin wrote, "modernity must stand under the sign of
that suicide which places its seal upon a heroic will," that can
apply not only to the tragic circumstances of Benjamin's own
self-destruction but also to the growing possibility of a planetary
suicide inherent in modernity's nuclear arms race. If the twentieth century vaunts an ideology of life, liberty, and the pursuit
of happiness, then critical theory poses the uncomfortable question of why no other century has witnessed such massive destruction of human life by human beings; or, in Walter Jens's imagery, "Is it really progress when cannibals use knives and
forks?"[10]

Innocent criticism as not knowing its own presuppositions
turns out to be guilty, drenched in the blood of its own heroic
hubris. There are, if you will, two dimensions of critical theory's
unmasking of innocent critique: the theological and methodological. More accurately, these are different aspects of the same
central thrust of critical theory; a refusal to cut off further relevant questions even when they lead us into the darkness of negativity. Where the more classical period of critical theory—embodied in the writings of Horkheimer, Adorno, Benjamin,
Marcuse, Fromm, Arendt—offers more clues to theological aspects, the contemporary writings of Jürgen Habermas and
American critical theory are much more explicitly methodological. I shall discuss briefly each of these in turn and, toward the
end of the chapter, suggest their underlying unity.

In seeking to unmask the archaic barbarism which hovers
within modernity as its shadow substance, critical theory in its
classic phase is often misunderstood as just another form of elit-
ist cultural resentment against modern mass culture. Conservatives misunderstand it as another legitimation of their fears of
social and cultural change. Liberals see in it a rear-guard protest
futilely raging against industrialization. Radicals view it as a betrayal of Marxism due to its failure to give foundational preeminence to a critique of political economy. What these three

counterpositions fail to grasp, each in its own peculiar way, is how critical theory is rooted in a commitment to contradiction which refuses to blink before the jeopardy of human destiny, because that commitment is a profound hope *against* hope. Against the conservative hope of restoring some semblance of balancing contradictions after the fashion of the eighteenth-century's *ancien régime,* critical theory hopefully despairs. Against the liberal hope of engineering contradictions after the fashion of nineteenth-century industrialization and urbanization, critical theory hopefully despairs. Against the radical hope of exploiting contradictions for the sake of revolutionary resolutions after the fashion of twentieth-century state socialisms, critical theory hopefully despairs.[11]

The mysticism of Benjamin is possible only for those who, like him, realize how Kafka's sickness unto death incarnates the reality of our crucial contradiction more adequately than does Kierkegaard. Only through Marx was such a mysticism meaningful. For only Marx's historical materialism dared to take responsibility in praxis for the humanization of divinity envisioned by Feuerbach. And only praxis reveals the abiding contradiction hopefully embedded within the very core of a project which dared to unite history and materialism. Benjamin's is a theology transformatively *within*—and not just extrinsic to—historical materialism which, he realized, will be successful only to the extent that "it takes theology into its service even if, as is well known today, theology is small and ugly, not risking itself to be seen in public."[12] If Marx's famous *Theses on Feuerbach* have become programmatic for the secularism of modern praxis, Benjamin's *Theses on the Philosophy of History* are paradigmatic for a spirituality nurtured within, and unafraid of, the genuinely human and religious needs which, if followed in praxis, will heal the biases of historical materialism.

Adorno also recognized the theological dimension of critical theory. Early in his own intellectual formation he was impressed with Ernst Bloch's *Geist der Utopie* with its dialectical mediation of human subjectivety and social objectivity; a mediation inspired by a persistent refusal to sacrifice the "unformulatable questions" at the heart of utopian aspirations to the pedestrian and banal restrictions of any purely formal logic.[13] Adorno's life-long friendship with Paul Tillich, who directed his *Habilita-tionsschrift* at Frankfurt, was at least an indication of how a Christian theologian could appreciate the theologically Jewish insights inspiring the work of Marxists like Bloch, Adorno, and Horkheimer. In his last letter to Bloch, Tillich wrote shortly before his death: "Finiteness permitting only hope against hope has laid hold of me."[14] Adorno encouraged Benjamin to hold fast to the creative contradiction, the tension between the two seeming opposites of theology and Marxism, as a "radicalization of the dialectic into the very glowing core of theology" which "would at the same time have to mean an utmost intensification of the social-dialectical, indeed, economic motifs."[15] Adorno's debates with Benjamin centered around those texts of the latter where Adorno judged that this dialectical tension was temporarily lost sight of in favor of simple one-to-one correlations between theological and Marxist categories. In those instances he warned Benjamin that theology degenerates into magic and Marxism into positivism.[16]

For Adorno only critical theory could provide the foundations for a hopeful redemptive critique in the midst of despair. In 1947 he wrote:

> The only philosophy which can be responsibly practiced in face of despair is the attempt to view all things as they would present themselves from the standpoint of redemption.[17]

It would not be far off the mark to suggest that Adorno's negative dialectics sought to explicate the horizon within which the creative contradiction of theology and Marxism could issue in redemptive critique. Marx's critique of religion presumed that theology could only be "bad theory" and had been sublated in the absolute knowledge of Hegel's philosophy. Hence to unmask the identity idealism of Hegel was for Marx to remove any worldly basis for religion or theology since a consistent unmasking of idealistic identity between reason and reality involved a socioeconomic critique of the irrationality of social reality in capitalism. Revolutionary praxis, by doing away with the real oppression of humankind, would realize or actualize an identity between reason and reality; such praxis would restore heart and soul to the social world and so render religion and theology useless insofar as religion "is the sigh of the oppressed creature, the heart of a heartless world and the soul of a soulless condition."[18] For Marx, therefore, his entire economic project was a critical attempt to materialize in real social relations the identity between reason and reality which had been abstractly, and hence falsely, presented in bourgeois idealism.[19] The actualization of philosophy would sublate philosophy (and by implication, theology) in a socialized humanity.

Critical theory agreed with the dialectical thrust of Marx's critique of any abstract identity between reason and reality. But it rejected as *simpliste* the claim that the state socialism of communism was in the process of sublating that nonidentity between reason and reality. The tragedies of modernity are traceable to a fatal flaw, a ghastly impatience with nonidentity and the negativity of finitude. Adorno and, in more measured tones, Horkheimer warn us that we must dwell in the negativity revealed by the great prophetic geniuses of our time, that we must resist the temptation to trade in their heritage for the mess of identity-potage their epigones dish out. Nor can we shirk our responsibility to criticize the prophetic geniuses themselves when they slip from the demands of nonidentity. For the horrors of claiming the identity of reason and reality are not some speculative nonsense of concern only to academics:

> Genocide is the absolute integration. It is on its way wherever men are leveled off—"polished off" as the German military called it—until one exterminates them literally, as deviations from the concept of their total nullity. Auschwitz confirmed the philosopheme of pure identity as death.[20]

For Adorno and Horkheimer Auschwitz is not an aberration from the process of civilization but an exaggeration of a more or less latent hubris seeking to impose identity and inherent in socialization as historically experienced till now.

The nonidentity of God and the world was emphasized by the

Jewish negative theology: there can be no images of God and his name cannot be uttered. Christianity emphasized how the transcendent God was immanent in the world through Christ. But it too preserved negative theology: in Christ God was identified with the powerless and the poor, with those nonidentified with "the world" and called to a mysterious Kingdom of God. But religious people did not live in such negativity. They began to identify the Kingdom of God with the Christian churches, they identified Christ with the mighty and powerful. Against this deadly (e.g., crusades, wars of religion) identification prophets and reformers rose up, but increasingly to less and less avail. Against the excesses and repressions of a decadent Christendom reason gradually asserted itself as nonidentical with established faith, as against the stifling identity system. At first, reason took the form of empirical rationality indicating how nature was *not* operating according to the identity patterns of the system. The success of the natural sciences soon spread to the study of man and society. Here too empirical rationality acted as a champion of nonidentity inasmuch as the incipient sociology (e.g., Comte) and psychology (e.g., Freud) raised further relevant questions challenging the status quo of the *ancien régime*. As long as an empirically oriented psychology and sociology—or empirically oriented human studies in general—challenged the hegemony of an "abstract," authoritarian universality whether in Christianity (e.g., the object of Enlightenment *philosophes* and Comte's criticisms) or in emergent bourgeois civilization (e.g., Freud's *Civilization and its Discontents*), they performed important critical roles. Empirical science and scholarship called attention to the plurality of concrete particulars not identifiable with the cultural conceptualism and uniformity of the status quo.

The liberally critical thrust of empirical rationality, however, gave birth to new social and cultural forms of repressive identity systems in capitalist industrialization. The old order of sacral hierarchy gave way to a new order of secular bureaucracy in which the myth of identity between reason and reality would be legitimated by an empirical science increasingly constituted by value-free (e.g., Weber) observation and quantification as the only valid form of rationality.[21] The critical insights of Comte or

Weber would be conceptualized into the social functionalism of Parsons. The emancipatory thrust of psychotherapy would be turned into many techniques of "adjustment" to social "reality" which would be anything but therapeutically liberating. Marx launched critical theory by practicing a new form of dialectical analysis which exposed the basic economic contradictions inherent in capitalist relations of production. He uncovered the contradictory nonidentity between the industrializing forces of production and the capitalist relations of production as the infrastructure capable of dialectically exposing the legal, political, cultural, and religious contradictions in modern society. As Marcuse wrote:

> In a society whose totality was determined by economic relations to the extent that the uncontrolled economy controlled all human relations, even the noneconomic was contained in the economy.[22]

Even this dialectical reason in Marx, however, became incorporated into an identity system of state socialism as Engels, Lenin, and Stalin successively reduced its critical-dialectical power into the platitudes of an empirically manipulated infrastructure controlled by party strategy and bureaucracy.[23] The early fears of critical theorists have been borne out by subsequent events wherein the apparent contradiction between late capitalism and state socialism tends to mask the underlying commitments of both to identity domination. Today they offer us the cynical choice between monopoly controlled states or state controlled monopolies. Marcuse caught well the dilemma of critical theory's relation to Marxism when, in his *Soviet Marxism: A Critical Analysis*, he pondered the paradox of how "the means for liberation and humanization operate for preserving domination and submission, and the theory that destroyed all ideology is used for the establishment of a new ideology."[24] In the light of this fatal identity flaw corrupting the critical potential of both religious and secular attempts at liberation, it was not philosophical pessimism so much as critical realism which led Horkheimer to assert in 1970 that Schopenhauer was correct in understanding the Judaeo-Christian teachings about original sin as accurate symbols of fateful human destiny in history.[25]

If Bloch and Benjamin explored the theological imagery conveying these inverse insights into the nonidentity of history, the other members of the Frankfurt School tended instead to articulate the methodological presuppositions of critique. Benjamin's comparison of theology to a wise but "ugly dwarf" which dared not "show its face in public" indicated how the task of critical theory consisted not in any direct use of theological or philosophical criticism, but in exploring the methodological foundations for that spring of nonidentity which, however fragile, had to be guarded against the inroads of identity thought and practice. The tragic destiny of Marxism meant that it too was not immune from the fatal flaw; hence the tendency of critical theory not to engage directly in the economic aspects of dialectical reason. If the first challenge of critical theory was the hopeful despair with which it unmasked the guilt of criticism innocent of its own presuppositions, then its second challenge would be to delve into those presuppositions—even when this meant charting very unfamiliar terrain.

In her excellent book, *The Origin of Negative Dialectics,* Susan Buck-Morss not only charts the early journey of the Frankfurt School but indicates the spirit in which it was undertaken. What she writes of Adorno applies as well to the other critical theorists:

> The whole point of his relentless insistence on negativity was to resist repeating in thought the structures of domination and reification that existed in society, so that instead of reproducing reality, consciousness could be critical, so that reason would recognize its own nonidentity with social reality, on the one hand, and material nature's nonidentity with the categorizing consciousness that passed for rationality, on the other.[26]

Although there is no set of methodological principles common to the proponents of critical theory—beyond the common nonidentity of each being on his or her own responsibility to truth—I believe certain features of their very individual approaches and methods can be formulated. These features indicated how their fidelity to dialectics as initiated by Marx demanded that they go beyond Marx—the issue being not just to interpret Marx but to change his theory to the extent that like him critical theory is committed to the liberation of human destiny.

The basic methodological presupposition of critical theory is that there should be a continual effort to realize reason in social reality. In this it goes beyond idealism and empiricism insofar as both of these apparent opposites take for granted that reason is identical with reality. Idealism and empiricism differ only in how that identity is known. Critical theory, however, views this debate as deceptive (*Schein*) inasmuch as the apparent opposites really agree on the fundamental identity of reason and reality. We have already mentioned this in regard to modernity. The modern is supposed to be the new, yet it is only by appreciating how modernity is in fact an ever-identical archaism that it is possible to discover what is different and new. The effort to realize reason in society means that critical theory is committed to the imperative value of truth. Truth as a correspondence between reason and reality is *not yet* attained—they are nonidentical—and so the task of truth is a questing and questioning after an ever more adequate realization of reason in reality. As Horkheimer put it, critical theory

> is motivated today by the effort really to transcend the tension and to abolish the opposition between the individual's purposefulness, spontaneity and rationality, and those work-process relationships on which society is built. Critical thought understands man as in conflict with himself until this opposition is removed. If activity governed by reason is proper to man, then existent social practice, which forms the individual's life down to its least details, is inhuman, and this inhumanity affects everything that goes on in the society.[27]

To transcend the tension of nonidentity between reason and reality means to hope in what Horkheimer calls "an obscure harmony between being and thought, understanding and sense perception," out of which "there will emerge in the future age the relation between rational intention and realization."[28]

If the "obscure harmony" is a hope and desire, an imperative to transform, then critical theory insists that this hope or desire be rooted in a profound insight into how contemporary social reality is irrational. This is not some type of idealist pessimism, which would be a total negation of rationality in contemporary social reality, but is an explicitation of what Marx termed "determinate negations." There is an unwillingness on the part of contemporary societies—whether in late capitalist or state-socialist forms—to realize the possibilities for human freedom and human education immanent in the developments of industrialization and technology. These latter, as forces of production, can be responsibly used for the humanization of society and the world only insofar as the relations of production, i.e., the relations of human beings with nature and with one another, are constituted by intelligent openness and critical responsibility. Critical theory aims at negating the flight from intelligence and responsibility so rampant in the so-called rationality of modern societies. Marx had hoped that the forces of production would necessarily lead to a change or revolution in the relations of production. Capitalism would progress to a point at which its own breakdown would be assured by the inner contradictions between the forces it was realizing and the relations of private property and maximization of profit it futilely attempted to maintain. Critical theory could no longer understand this determinate negation as "necessarily" occurring, as though Marx had discovered "iron laws of social history" which would make him, as one reviewer of *Das Kapital* had dubbed him, "the Darwin of historical change." The subsequent history of Marxism belied such a necessity, as well as the subsequent history of capitalism.

The determinate negation of critical theory had to link more closely the development of reason and the development of freedom. This allied critical theory "to certain ancient truths," as Marcuse stated, for human beings "can be more than a manipulable subject in the production process of a class society."[29] The ancient truths—to summarize the work in this area of Horkheimer, Hannah Arendt, and Jürgen Habermas—involved critical theory in a transposition of the classic Greek distinctions between theory, praxis, and technique. Theory, for the Greeks and medieval scholastics, aimed at necessary and immutable laws of the cosmos, and the prime embodiment of theory was metaphysics. Praxis was human action, involving human deeds and speech, and was aimed at the prudent guidance of contingent human and political affairs. Technique was human production or making, as embodied in craftsmanship, and aimed at the control and manipulation of natural material toward production. With the collapse of pre-Enlightenment religious and metaphysical world views, theory shifted from metaphysics to mathematics and technique. The theoretical enlightenment of the Graeco-Roman and medieval worlds subordinated praxis and technique as subaltern modes of knowing to metaphysical theory. The modern enlightenment, on the contrary, has tended to subordinate theory and praxis to technique as the natural and human sciences were increasingly absorbed into the methods of technology and production. In this fateful subordination modern empirical-analytical sciences, as well as social-historical sciences, developed what Horkheimer has called "traditional theory" as opposed to "critical theory." It is traditional since it unintentionally carried over the presuppositions of classical theory, not in terms of metaphysics, but in terms now of necessary, intelligible laws or regularities in nature and society which modern science aimed at disclosing through statistical induction and mathematical-symbolic deduction or constructions. It is, however, more dangerous and destructive in its modern form as "instrumental rationality" since it is no longer merely theoretical but engaged, through scientism and technocracy, in forcing physical and human nature into its manipulating conceptual categories.[30]

This "scientistic consciousness," as Habermas calls it, has many implications. Methodology is misunderstood as a Cartesian quest for indubitable certitude and as consisting in axiomatic techniques which can be applied more or less automatically.[31] In philosophy there are efforts either to make all thought conform to the techniques of the natural sciences as closely as possible (e.g., positivism, empiricism, naturalism, logicism, linguistic analysis of the Vienna circle, historicism, structuralism) or to preserve some domain for philosophy which *per impossibile* would not be invaded by the sciences (e.g., idealism, later Husserlian and post-Husserlian phenomenology, existentialism, personalism). The human sciences such as psychology and sociology are increasingly marked by similar dichotomies between empiricist and idealist orientations, e.g., the debates between behaviorism and humanism, functionalism and symbolic interactionism, sociobiologism and anthropologicism. The determinate negation of such philosophical and scientific-methodological dichotomies has engaged critical theory in the project of laying foundations for a new enlightenment, one in which praxis as specifically human performance and communication would provide the criteria for a nonalienating science and technology. Theory of itself is inadequate for this task since its drive for coherence and system, as is well illustrated in Hegel's absolute knowledge (*Begriff*), tends to reflect and promote an imposition of identity categories upon natural and social reality. Only a critical theory, that is a theorizing which is attentive to its own operations as praxis and open to correction in the light of that praxis, can free methodology, philosophy, the sciences, and technology from present dehumanizations in society and ecology. Such a praxis enlightenment attends to the "obscure harmony" between intelligence and phantasy in such a way as to promote freedom and responsibility.[32] This means that intelligence and phantasy, as nonidentical, afford a creative tension in which the particular and concrete provide the matrix for insight, understanding, and action. Thus Adorno speaks of the need for "exact phantasy" which allows the unique nonidentity of objects to reveal their particularity and through this particularity their relations to a yet-to-be discovered totality.[33] Attentiveness to phantasy dismantles the rigidity of a conceptualistic intentionality which forces its prejudices on reality—a process not only found in Husserlian phenomenology but also in technocracy.[34]

This praxis enlightenment aims at freeing us from the alienating domination of past and present. The exact phantasy, if attended to critically and creatively, mediates future possibilities undiscovered in the past or present.[35] While Marcuse explored the atrophication of phantasy in *One Dimensional Man* and *Eros and Civilization,* it was a constant theme of Adorno, Horkheimer, and others in their criticisms of the mass culture industry.[36] The irony of mass culture is that it seems to thrive on images. Advertising and the mass media are, however, conveyors of packaged images and symbols; their motto might be, "Leave nothing to the imagination." The apotheosis of this trend is pornography; the real is the already-out-there now which has only to be looked at to be known and consumed. This atrophies phantasy inasmuch as it bends it to the imperious demands of conceptual technique. Nowhere is this more evident than in the omnipresent standardization of life in consumerist societies. The particular and unique are destroyed for the sake of a kind of conceptualist uniformity—as though Platonic ideas were being packaged and consumed: if you've seen one neon-cluttered main street you've seen them all; if you've eaten one Big Mac you've eaten them all, and so on ad infinitum. Nature, both physical and human, rebels against this "bad materialization of idealism"—as Marcuse termed it—as is now becoming evident in ecological pollution and human disease.[37]

Critical theory is the exact opposite of such a bad materialism. Phantasy and concept cannot be related in a one-to-one mechanical way as though phantasy mirrors sense experience and concepts mirror phantasy. Nor were critical theorists satisfied with more recondite philosophical epistemologies or cognitional theories—Descartes, Kant, Hegel, Dilthey, Husserl, to mention only some of the major proponents they investigated and found wanting. Marx does provide an important orientation insofar as he calls attention to the social conditioning of phantasy and intelligence; at the same time, he insists that phantasy and intelligence can and do transcend that conditioning insofar as they become critically reflective. The liberating praxis of critical or dialectical reason draws its criteria, according to Marcuse, from its own "transcendent project." Its project both exposes the contradictions in the existing social totality and projects how those contradictions can be resolved in a higher or more humane and free social order.[38] Erich Fromm explored this transcending project in the field of social psychology. Jürgen Habermas has attempted to elaborate a foundational methodology in terms of praxis as performative human communication capable of orienting the empirical-analytic sciences and the historical-hermeneutical sciences toward the emancipatory interests of critical theory. Habermas's reformulation of the transcendental project is in terms of what he calls three distinct "quasi-transcendental" interests guiding and constituting three distinct forms of knowledge. The *technical* interest in controlling and instrumentalizing action guides the empirical-analytical sciences, which include both the natural sciences and those social sciences interested in nomological (i.e., technically utilizable) knowledge; this technical interest aims at the reproduction of human life through labor. The *practical* interest in the survival of social and cultural histories guides the historical-hermeneutical sciences, which include the humanities as well as the historical and social sciences inasmuch as they are interested in symbolically meaningful interaction. The *emancipatory* interest in gaining for humankind more effective and responsible freedom guides the critically oriented sciences such as psychoanalysis, critical social theory, and philosophy understood as a reflective and critical philosophy of history with practical intent. These three quasi-transcendental interests (Habermas uses "quasi" in order to emphasize that he is not understanding the interests in terms of an idealist transcendental philosophy) have their basis in the natural history of the species in terms of labor, language, and power (*Herrschaft* or power as domination). While all three cognitive interests are different dimensions or aspects of social evolution as learning processes, the emancipatory interest attempts to preserve critical theory's link between reason and freedom by indicating how these learning processes presuppose and aim at intersubjective communication undistorted by individual, group, or social biases.[39]

This development of the transcendental project within critical theory, from Marcuse and the early critical theorists through Fromm to Habermas, has not been by any means smooth or without internal criticism. Adorno and Marcuse chided Fromm's later use of categories from Karen Horney, Harry S. Sullivan, and others as a slippage into "Freudian revisionism." This criticism was made inasmuch as Fromm began to assume noncontingent, basic human needs which seemed to abandon his earlier attempts to essay a cross-fertilization of Marx and Freud by expanding the latter's interest in individual histories of pathology to include a Marxist class analysis.[40] In a somewhat similar vein, Habermas's distinction of the three quasi-transcendental cognitive interests has been criticized for separating what Marx had joined together. Specifically, the call for a transformation of science and technology away from an instrumental domination of nature and society in the writings of Adorno, Horkheimer, and Marcuse seems to be abandoned by Habermas. While the latter's differentiation of cognitive interests would check the totalizing identity-thrust of "instrumental rationality" and scientism, it also has the explicit effect of legitimating labor as intrinsically informed by the technical interest in control. As Habermas has stated: "Realizing this, it is impossible to envisage how ... we could renounce technology, more particularly our technology, in favor of a qualitatively different one."[41]

There is, however, a deeper criticism of Habermas; one which calls into question not only his work but the entire thrust of critical theory itself. It is a criticism that is very much on the minds of American critical theorists.

### The Challenge to Critical Theory

The basic criticism of Habermas's reconstruction of historical materialism in terms of communication theory and quasi-transcendental interests is that the thrust of his critical theory identifies no clearly defined target group as a potential agent for social transformation. The quasi-transcendental interests are common to the entire human species in its physical, social, cultural, political histories of reproduction as learning processes. The emancipatory interest in constraint-free communication does not provide the *immediate* foundations for critical sociopolitical criticism and action. Thus, at the end of his admirable study, *The Critical Theory of Jürgen Habermas*, Thomas McCarthy can write:

> In the absence of an identifiable "agent of social transformation," he [Habermas] is forced to remain at the social level of pointing out broad crisis tendencies intrinsic to the structure of advanced capitalism. His critique retains an anonymous character, addressed to "mankind as such" and thus to no group in particular.[42]

McCarthy goes on to draw the parallels with the founding members of the Frankfurt School, indicating how Habermas is, perhaps, less pessimistic than they were insofar as he has succeeded in pointing out in new ways how nonidentity is present in the very mechanisms of identity formation in the "total society" of advanced capitalism.

> In support of this contention he has met the contemporary sciences of man on their own fields and shaped them into a critical consciousness of the age. No better example could be found for Bloch's dictum: "reason cannot flourish without hope, hope cannot speak without reason."[43]

A similar tone can be found at the end of Susan Buck-Morss's study on *The Origins of Negative Dialectics* where she indicates how the stringent articulation of negative dialectics in Adorno led to his insistence upon "nonparticipation" even in revolutionary movements in order to keep alive the capacity for experiencing the nonidentical.

> Hence, in the name of revolution, thought could never acknowledge a revolutionary situation; in the name of utopia, it could never work for utopia's realization. Adorno ensured perhaps too successfully that reason did not become "instrumental." For instrumental reason preserved a moment of "use value" which negative dialectics had to abandon. The result was that as opposites, they too converged: instrumental reason lost sight of rational goals, ceased to be a means, and became an end in itself; but negative dialectics abrogated political utility, and thus became an end in itself as well.[44]

Critical theory's unmasking of innocent critique as guilty seemed only to lead to a practice of theorizing confined—like Benjamin's descriptions of the bourgeois *intérieur*—to a futile substitution of writing for action. In 1968 Horkheimer himself acknowledged the intent of such criticisms while offering only a slight consolation to those really dedicated to realizing the import of critical theory in praxis.

> Men of good will want to draw conclusions for political action from the critical theory. Yet there is no fixed

method for doing this; the only universal prescription is
that one must have insight into one's own responsibility.
Thoughtless and dogmatic application of the critical theory to practice in changed historical circumstances can
only accelerate the very process which the theory aimed
at denouncing. All those seriously involved in the critical
theory, including Adorno, who developed it with me, are
in agreement on this point.[45]

Some will find this as disconcerting as Habermas's admonitions
to the German students ten years ago: they wanted a new society and he urged them to begin with a well thought out plan
for university reform.[46]

The reception of critical theory in North America, however,
shows signs of developing a critical mediation between the
methodological concerns of its German and European counterparts and sociopolitical transformation. The new left of the early
1960s—which Stanley Aronowitz has characterized as "a movement without theory, a rebellion without awareness either of its
traditions or interests"—failed to appreciate how it presupposed
the viability of the so-called democratic institutions already in
place. The student radicals of those days accepted the myth of
popular participation and thought that by massive demonstra-
tions the people could wrest the government from the control of
the military-industrial complex. Those who read Marcuse failed
to understand his transcendental project as a critique of the instrumental rationality which could (and eventually did) convert
the counterculture into a merchantable product for Madison Avenue. Their "action critique of modern American society and
culture failed to extend to the cognitive spheres."[47] Increasingly
the new left of the 60s found their energies dissipated by a veritable consumerism of radical issues. Without a serious cognitive
and systemic analysis of late capitalism as an identity-whole,
they tried desperately to remedy now this symptom and now
that. It is of little surprise, therefore, that in the frustrations of
the 1970s some turned to critical theory in order to retrieve a
genuinely Marxist critique of late capitalism. The fruits of that
retrieval are now beginning to appear; in the remainder of this

chapter I shall sketch some of their economic, methodological, and theological contributions.

Critical theorists have always been chided by both Marxists and liberals for their neglect of a thoroughgoing appropriation of economic critique. To the extent that such criticisms originated from either a state-socialist fundamentalism on the infra-suprastructure misunderstanding of Marx or a technocratic instrumentalization of cultural critique in late capitalism, the criticisms were easily dismissed—perhaps too easily.[48] American critical theorists, inspired by the works of such analysts as Marc Linder, Paul Baran, Paul Sweezy, and Harry Braverman have begun to articulate the relationships between the cultural Marxism of critical theory and Marx's own critique of political economy.[49] Central to this work is an understanding and reformulation of Marx's insights into the dynamics of capitalist accumulation. Much too briefly stated, Marx articulated the intrinsic contradictions in capitalist accumulation in terms of barriers immanent in capital to an ever expanding rate of profit. "The real barrier to capital is capital itself," as he pointedly phrased it.[50] The barrier is in the forces of production, but capitalism thrives on material (humankind's relation to nature) and social (interrelationships of human beings) relations of production which futilely attempt to ignore those limits and offset the inevitable falling rate of profit. Julius Sensat's *Habermas and Marxism: An Appraisal* explores this phenomenon as analyzed by both Marx and Habermas. He—correctly in my judgment—retrieves a Marxian analysis which is more adequate to an understanding of late capitalism than Habermas's too rigid distinctions between technical interests and practical interests would permit.[51] Trent Schroyer's *The Critique of Domination: The Origins and Development of Critical Theory* outlines some of the main political and social consequences of efforts in American capitalism to hold off the falling rate of profit, or the phases of "disaccumulation" as Schroyer terms them. There are the political economic consequences—Keynesianism—of increasing governmental intervention into the economy through deficit financing and massive pork barrel projects farmed out to private industries. These become coupled with ever greater military budgets and the quest for foreign markets secured by military and/or economic "stabilization programs." As corporations committed to an illusory ever expanding rate of profit team up with governments to secure such multinational markets, the American home front is marked by an increasing instrumental rationalization of society. The first victim, as classical critical theorists saw, is politics itself. There is a widespread depoliticization of society as reasoned public debate on fundamental issues is ignored in favor of a party system dedicated to act as a buffer zone between competing interest groups and corporate power.[52] A major futility of this buffer role can be seen in the contradictory governmental spendings for high, capital intensive technological research, on the one hand, and huge welfare subsidies for the unemployed, on the other. As Schroyer observes: "The very existence of a *political* process is today questionable and it is perhaps more accurately viewed as a planning mechanism for the economy and a service delivery system for the needs of organizable groups."[53]

A promising feature of American critical theorists' efforts to retrieve central insights in Marx's critique of political economy is their openness to further very relevant questions on the production process and monetary circulation due to changing historical situations. Marx emphasized the nonidentity between forces and relations of production in early capitalism. The massive political and social efforts to suppress that nonidentity have not only characterized the subsequent developments of capitalism but have also characterized the technocratic and authoritarian tendencies in state socialisms.[54] In the light of this, it

> is necessary to reopen the question left unanswered by the socialist tradition in both theory and practice: what are the processes that can create a social system in which individual and social development can be reconciled without generating a highly centralized and authoritarian system? This question cannot be approached theoretically, but requires a deeper understanding of historical processes.[55]

This implies a retrieval of Marx which decisively critiques the reductionist tendencies of so much supposedly orthodox Marxist economics. The nonidentity between the economic realities of production processes and existing capitalist *and* socialist economic theories cannot be overcome by the conceptualistic techniques of trying to force those realities into positivist-capitalist or socialist-idealist categories. "No self-selected vanguard can express the goals or in any sense 'make' the preconditions for revolutionary change by the use of instrumental Marxist-Leninist science."[56] The similarities and differences between late capitalism and state socialism in regard to both the surplus accumulation phases and basic distribution phases of the production processes and monetary circulation should lead American critical theorists to analyze those phases more profoundly and more concretely in order to show how the forces of production require relations of production constituted by intelligent and responsibly effective freedom.[57] No amount of moralism or political rhetoric regarding class struggle can absolve us from this demanding task.

In the areas of critical methodology American critical theorists are providing significant advances on, and challenges to, European critical theory. Critical theory has always been harassed by a positivist effort to instrumentalize critique through posing the option of *either* late capitalism *or* state socialism. This instrumentalizes critique since it tries to subordinate it to the present supposed crux between capitalism and socialism as they de facto function. At least as strongly as their European counterparts, American critical theorists reject this as not really a choice but only a legitimatization of the status quo. Marx's critique of political economy is too important to become such dogmatism. The nonidentity between reason and reality means that the dialectical processes inherent in social reality concretely contradict the late capitalist and state socialist efforts to impose their respective conceptualities on those processes. More pointedly than European critical theorists, Americans are committed to a theoretical effort to understand the *concrete* social reality. Theory is not an impoverished abstraction away from that reality. Instead theory as critical is a profound effort to understand processive reality ever more adequately. Theory, then, does not move away from the concrete, only to be returned to it in the form of some sort of practical application. Instead, theory is continually moving toward the complexity of the concrete and, in the measure that it is correct in indicating the underlying concrete and contradictory tensions in reality, it is capable of guiding the transformation of reality. This orientation of American critical theory takes its inspiration from Marx's own methodology.[58]

Hence the methodological significance of American critical theory is strategic as well. The alienation of Marxism in state socialism requires what Schroyer calls "the self-formation of a critical intelligentsia" as intrinsic to social transformation. The struggles for liberation now in process must be supported and deepened by this development of critical intelligence which aims at showing how they are transforming the relations of production.[59] While this has worldwide significance in terms of the struggle against economic multinational domination and exploitation, it also is very relevant in terms of the self-formation of critical intelligence within the American educational system. For the latter not only exhibits the cultural contradictions of capitalism but, as Bowles and Gintis have shown, the economic contradictions as well.[60] These will only become more evident in the coming two decades; it will be less and less possible to cover over the irrationalities in society and education. This only underscores the importance of American critical theory in retrieving not only Marx but also the possibilities for critical collaboration with all fields of human cognitive activity.[61] Many works are contributions toward such a critical collaboration.

Richard Bernstein has essayed dialectical retrievals of European and Anglo-American social and political philosophies, indicating the elements of nonidentity which correlated them with the transcendental project of critical theory.[62] Alvin Gouldner has shown how academic sociology in both North America and Russia has generally been instrumentalized into a functionalism inattentive to its own inherent anomie. His more recent work on the dark side of dialectics explores the possibilities for social transformation in the nonidentities between the commitments of intellectual communities to raise further relevant questions and the fears of these commitments encrusted in the institutions of late capitalism and state socialism.[63] Christopher Lasch's works on the family and the narcissism of contemporary culture provide correctives to, and extensions of work done in, European critical theory by indicating the massive nonidentity between the personal and cultural values cherished in conservative and liberal traditions, on the one hand, and how those values are systemically undermined by the economic, political, and cultural forces those traditions support, on the other hand.[64]

The significance of these works consists in the elements they assemble for showing how the contradictions between the forces and relations of production are capable of being read in the philosophical, cultural, political, and personal contradictions in late capitalism and state socialism. They indicate how the dialectical nonidentity between reason and reality Marx had explored within the infrastructure of forces and relations of production can also be explored within the suprastructure of cultural and social processes. The challenge to American critical theory which these and similar works pose is to move beyond more limited questions on the Kantian, Hegelian, or Freudian presuppositions of such works to the methodologically basic issues the performance of such critique presupposes. The recognition of a whole series of nonidentity between reason and reality that does not fall into a kind of ontological pessimism—as though reality itself were intrinsically irrational—but instead insists upon the hope and desire continually to strive to overcome that nonidentity demands that we go beyond the "obscure harmony" between being and thought, between phantasy and reason, to the internally related and recurrent concrete activities operative in both cognitive criticism and historically transformative action.[65] The methodological challenges facing contemporary critical theory is that the conceptual categories of all previous cognitive positions and counterpositions are fundamentally inadequate to elucidate the actual performance of critical theory today. Late capitalism as a bad materialization of idealism and state socialism as a bad idealization of materialism should at least warn us of a fatal oversight inherent in all previous methodologies employed by social criticism. To the degree that the actual performance of social criticism has been much better than the methodologies to which criticism cognitively appealed, to that degree the nonidentity between method and critique should be intelligently and responsibly investigated. Only such investigations would enable critical theory to contribute to overcoming the alienation of method operative in both scientism or technocracy and antiscientific or antitechnological existentialism. The forces of science and technology contradict the methodological relations of science and technology expressed in positivism and idealism.[66]

The economic and methodological challenges to develop further critical theory require attention also to theological challenges. The end of innocent critique implies the recognition that determinate negation in critique cannot be allowed to slip into a totalizing negation so characteristic of identity systems. To the extent that this occurred in the Marxist critique of religion it contributed to the alienating transition from hierarchic *sacralist* authoritarianism to bureaucratic *secularist* authoritarianism. Sacralism and secularism then confront one another as illusory opposites, whereas in fact they both share in the root alienation of attempting to maintain identity systems. Sacralist theism and secularist atheism are no more contradictory than late capitalism and state socialism: the illusion of a god identical with ecclesial-social institutions is merely replaced with the illusion of a humankind identical with political-economic institutions. Both types of identification are attempts to repress or deny the nonidentity constitutive of *both* genuine experience of God *and* genuine experience of human freedom. When Marx wrote that "the presupposition of all critique is the critique of religion," he scarcely understood how or why his statement would be truer than his intention.[67] He rather innocently believed that in criticizing the idealism of Hegel and civil society he had also criticized religion and theology. He believed rather innocently that all that was required was to put into practice the Feuerbachian inverse projection.[68] The innocence of secularist faith can no

longer be sustained, any more than the innocence of a sacralist
faith could be sustained. Both types of faith—sacralist and secularist—have given abundant evidence of a hubris all too guilty of
crucifying both God and humankind. But the reality of God and
of humankind continually demonstrates that it is nonidentical
with the conceptualities which try so futilely to destroy and en-
tomb it. Just as the reality of economic processes is nonidentical
with the false conceptualities rampant in late capitalism and
state socialism, just as the reality of science, technology, art,
scholarship, politics, and culture is nonidentical with the false
conceptualities of the many varieties of positivism and idealism,
so the reality of God and of humankind is nonidentical with the
false conceptualities of sacralism and secularism.

Many theologians are engaged in a critical analysis of how the
false conceptualities of sacralism and secularism distort the realities of religion and society. Similar to the early critical theorists,
they refuse to identify sacralist distortions of religious theory
and practice with the religious realities experienced in genuine
faith, hope, and love. The struggles of the poor and oppressed
throughout the world, and especially in so-called Third World
countries, indicate how religious meanings and values—and religious institutions—can be and are integral to those struggles
for effective human freedom.[69] The many forms of liberation
theology and political theology are developing the dialectical
and foundational criteria which are theologically operative in
such struggles. As these theologians point out, it is not a question
of compromising the religious scriptures and religious traditions
in order to "apply" such watered-down versions of religious
teachings to social and political struggles. Rather, it is a question
of showing how those human struggles for freedom reveal the
true meanings and values of the narratives and teachings of religion. It is a question of understanding how the watered-down
distortions in a sacralist authoritarianism and privatization of
religion have really failed to hand on the truth of religion.[70]
Methodologically, this has led theologians to enter into a critical
collaboration with many different types of contemporary science and critical scholarship.[71] This is beginning to sublate the
project of liberal theological scholarship. That project was con-

cerned with whether or not the historical-critical methods would negate the religious meanings and values of religious traditions. In a sense this problematic suffered from the innocent critique of instrumental rationality. The historical-critical methods were conceived as techniques which would show how religious meanings and values merely reflected the plausibility structures of the societies and cultures in which they were incarnated. This tended to identify those meanings and values with the societies and cultures, draining religion of its inherent transcendent project and promoting a liberalist historicism. The end of innocent criticism has meant theologically that such historical criticism has itself to be critized in the light of its own unexamined presuppositions. Theologians are now developing social-critical methods which indicate how religious scriptures and traditional doctrines do not merely reflect the societies or cultures of their origin but actually criticize the plausibility structures of those societies or cultures. They are nonidentical with the latter.[72]

This sublation of the historical-critical into the social-critical understanding of Judaeo-Christian scriptures and traditions does not try to reduce biblical messages to programs (moral or political) for enlightened social change. As Johann B. Metz and Helmut Peukert indicate, the apocalyptic nonidentity of critical theory is intensified in any genuinely theological dialectic of emancipation and redemption. Nor is a social-critical retrieval of Judaeo-Christian traditions indifferent or neutral in regard to the struggles for a more humane social order. Neither a spiritualized indifference nor a pragmatized reduction can do justice to the tension of nonidentity constitutive of imminent expectation of the Kingdom of God as immediately experienced in anamnetic solidarity with the dead and the victims, the outcasts and the powerless.[73] North American political theologians and Latin American liberation theologians are beginning to explore how the nonidentity constitutive of the struggles for freedom and justice reveals a religious immediacy at the heart of human solidarity in the quest for that "unmediated humanism" glimpsed by Marx.[74] This theological task goes to the very core of critical theory itself, intensifying its social-dialectical, and indeed economic, motifs.

## NOTES

1. Cf. Paul Piccone, "Beyond Identity Theory," in John O'Neil (ed.), *On Critical Theory* (New York: Seabury Press, 1976), pp. 129–42.

2. For example, in North America there are the following journals: *Catalyst, The Insurgent Sociologist, Kapitalistate, New German Critique, Telos: A Quarterly Journal of Radical Social Theory, Social Text, Theory and Society: Renewal and Critique in Social Theory.* Also available are British journals such as *Critique, New Left Review,* and *Radical Science Journal.*

3. Translations of European critical theorists have been published mainly by Seabury Press, Beacon Press, and Urizen Books. Among the best studies of critical theory by Americans are: Andrew Arato and Eike Gebhardt (eds.), *The Essential Frankfurt School Reader* (New York: Urizen Books, 1978); Richard Bernstein, *The Restructuring of Social and Political Theory* (New York: Harcourt, Brace, Jovanovich, 1976); Paul Connerton (ed.), *Critical Sociology* (New York: Penguin Books, 1976); Susan Buck-Morss, *The Origins of Negative Dialectics* (New York: The Free Press, 1977); Alvin Gouldner, *The Dialectic of Ideology and Technology* (New York: Seabury Press, 1976) and his *The Future of Intellectuals and the Rise of the New Class* (New York: Seabury Press, 1979); Bart Grahl and Paul Piccone (eds.), *Towards a New Marxism* (St. Louis: Telos Press, 1973); Dick Howard, *The Marxian Legacy* (New York: Urizen Books, 1977); Martin Jay, *The Dialectical Imagination* (Boston: Little, Brown & Company, 1973); Thomas McCarthy, *The Critical Theory of Jürgen Habermas* (Cambridge: MIT Press, 1978); John O'Neil (ed.), *On Critical Theory* (New York: Seabury Press, 1976); New Left Review, (eds.), *Western Marxism: A Critical Reader* (London: Verso, 1978); Trent Schroyer, *The Critique of Domination* (New York: George Braziller, 1973); Julius Sensat, *Habermas and Marxism* (Beverly Hills: Sage Publications, 1979); Andrew Feenberg, *Lukács, Marx and the Sources of Critical Theory* (Totowa, N.J.: Rowman & Littlefield, 1981); David Held, *Introduction to Critical Theory: Horkheimer to Habermas* (Berkeley: Univ. of California Press, 1980); Russell Keat, *The Politics of Social Theory* (Chicago: Univ. of Chicago Press, 1981); Garbis Kortian, *Metacritique: The Philosophical Argument of J. Habermas* (New York: Cambridge Univ. Press, 1980); John B. Thompson, *Critical Hermeneutics: A Study in the Thought of P. Ricoeur and J. Habermas* (New York: Cambridge Univ. Press, 1981).

4. Besides the above mentioned books there are a growing number

of English and American writers who critically use categories of Marxist origin in their work. For example, in theology there are the writings of Gregory Baum, John Coleman, Francis Fiorenza, Elizabeth Fiorenza, Herbert McCabe, Rudolf Siebert, Lee Cormie, not to mention the Latin American liberation theologians or the European political theologians. In political science there are the works of Michael Harrington, Irving Horowitz, Ralph Miliband; in education there is the recent work of Samuel Bowles and Herbert Gintis; in aesthetics and literary criticism, the works of Terry Eagleton, John Brenkman, Fredric Jameson, and those who write for the journals *Social Text* and *Praxis Four;* in social and cultural anthropology there are the works of thinkers like Christopher Lasch or Mark Poster; in economics those like Harry Braverman, Stanley Aronowitz, Robert Heilbroner, Paul Sweezy, G. William Domhoff, Maurice Dobb, Arun Bose; in psychology there are the writings of Erich Fromm, Bruce Brown, Richard King, Paul Robinson.

5. Besides the works of Bernstein, Gouldner, Howard, and Schroyer, mentioned above, cf. John McMurtry, *The Structure of Marx's World-View* (Princeton: University Press, 1978); David Noble, *America by Design* (New York: Knopf, 1977); Bertell Ollman, *Alienation* (Cambridge: University Press, 1971).

6. T. Adorno, "Reflexionen zur Klassentheorie" (1942), in his *Gesammelte Schriften,* vol. 8 (Frankfurt: Suhrkamp, 1972), p. 376.

7. Cf. Max Horkheimer and Theodor Adorno, *Dialectic of Enlightenment,* trans. John Cumming (New York: Herder & Herder, 1972); Buck-Morss, op. cit., pp. 43–62.

8. W. Benjamin, *Gesammelte Schriften,* vol. 1, 3 (Frankfurt: Suhrkamp, 1974), p. 1232; for a theological transposition of Benjamin's inverse insight, cf. Johann B. Metz, *Faith in History and Society* (New York: Seabury Press, 1979), pp. 169–83.

9. W. Benjamin, *Zur Kritik der Gewalt* (Frankfurt: Suhrkamp, 1965), pp. 84–85.

10. Walter Jens (ed.), *Warum ich Christ bin* (Munich: Piper, 1979), p. 11; also Benjamin, *Gesammelte Schriften,* vol. 1, 2 (Frankfurt: Suhrkamp, 1974), pp. 578f.; Buck-Morss, op. cit., pp. 165–84. Also G. Eliot, *Twentieth Century Book of the Dead* (New York: Scribner, 1972).

11. Cf. M. Jay, op. cit., pp. 253–80; on the conservative hope, cf. Richard Sennett, *The Fall of Public Man* (New York: Knopf, 1977); on the liberal hope, cf. Ernest Becker, *The Denial of Death* (New York: Free Press, 1973) and his *The Structure of Evil* (New York: George Braziller, 1968); on the radical hope, cf. Michael Albert and Robin Hahnel, *Unorthodox Marxism* (Boston: South End Press, 1978), Chris Harman, *Bureaucracy and Revolution in Eastern Europe* (London: Pluto Press, 1974), McMurtry, op. cit., pp. 157–87.

12. Benjamin, *Zur Kritik der Gewalt*, p. 78; on Kafka and Kierkegaard, cf. Buck-Morss, op. cit., pp. 114–21, 141–44. Marx's materialist conception of history—he never wrote of "historical materialism"—must be understood as over against Hegelian idealism. In that context Marx's materialist conception of history can be critically understood as an (admittedly inadequate) social correlative to the centrality of insight into phantasm as the origin of conceptualization. Cf. M. Lamb, *History, Method and Theology* (Missoula: Scholars Press, 1978), pp. 57–115, 485–506.

13. Cf. Buck-Morss, op. cit., p. 4.

14. Cf. Wilhelm and Marion Pauck, *Paul Tillich: His Life* (New York: Harper & Row, 1976), p. 282.

15. Adorno, *Über Walter Benjamin* (Frankfurt: Suhrkamp, 1970), p. 117.

16. Cf. Buck-Morss, op. cit., p. 157.

17. Adorno, *Minima Moralia: Reflections on the Damaged Life*, trans. E. Jephcott (London: New Left Books, 1974), p. 247.

18. Marx, *Critique of Hegel's Philosophy of Right*, trans. Joseph O'Malley (Cambridge: University Press, 1970), p. 131.

19. Cf. Joseph O'Malley, "Marx, Marxism and Method," in S. Avineri (ed.), *The Varieties of Marxism* (Hague: Nijhof, 1977), pp. 1–50; on theological critique, cf. F. van den Oudenrijn, *Kritische Theologie als Kritik der Theologie* (Mainz: Grünewald, 1972) and Johann B. Metz, *Faith in History and Society*.

20. Adorno, *Negative Dialectics*, trans. E. B. Ashton (New York: Seabury Press, 1973), p. 362; also M. Horkheimer, *Critique of Instrumental Reason*, trans. Matthew O'Connell (New York: Seabury Press, 1974).

21. Cf. Alvin Gouldner, *The Coming Crisis of Western Sociology* (New York: Avon Books, 1970); T. Adorno et al., *Der Positivismusstreit in der deutschen Soziologie* (Berlin: Luchterhand, 1969).

22. Marcuse, *Negations: Essays in Critical Theory*, trans. J. Shapiro (Boston: Beacon Press, 1968), p. 144.

23. Cf. books by Albert, Hahnel, Harman, and McMurtry in n. 11 above; also the Soviet reception of functionalism, Gouldner, *The Coming Crisis of Western Sociology*, pp. 447–77; and H. Marcuse, *Soviet Marxism: A Critical Analysis* (New York: Vintage Books, 1961).

24. Marcuse, ibid., p. xiv.

25. M. Horkheimer, *Die Sehnsucht nach dem ganz Anderen* (Hamburg: Furche Verlag, 1970), pp. 64f.

26. Buck-Morss, op. cit., p. 189.

27. Horkheimer, *Critical Theory*, trans. Matthew O'Connell (New York: Herder & Herder, 1972), p. 210.

28. Ibid., p. 217.

29. Marcuse, *Negations*, p. 153.

30. Horkheimer, *Critique of Instrumental Reason,* pp. 1–62; *Critical Theory,* pp. 188–252; also John Thompson, *Critical Hermeneutics,* pp. 71–111; and note the critical alternatives to instrumental rationality discussed in chap. 5 below.

31. Habermas, *Knowledge and Human Interests,* trans. J. Shapiro (Boston: Beacon Press, 1971), pp. 301–17; T. McCarthy, op. cit., pp. 1–125.

32. Cf. Marcuse, "Philosophy and Critical Theory" in *Negations,* pp. 134–58.

33. Cf. Buck-Morss, op. cit., pp. 85–88.

34. Ibid., pp. 63–81.

35. Marcuse, *Negations,* p. 155.

36. Cf. M. Jay, op. cit., pp. 173–218.

37. Cf. Horkheimer, *Eclipse of Reason* (New York: Seabury Press, 1974), pp. 3–127; H. Marcuse, *One-Dimensional Man* (Boston: Beacon Press, 1964), pp. 1–122.

38. Marcuse, ibid., pp. 203–57, esp. pp. 220ff.

39. Cf. T. McCarthy, op. cit., pp. 53–90, 272–357.

40. Cf. Arato and Gebhardt (eds.), *The Essential Frankfurt School Reader,* pp. 477–92; also McCarthy, op. cit., pp. 193–212.

41. Habermas, *Toward a Rational Society,* trans. J. Shapiro (Boston: Beacon Press, 1970), p. 87. Also McCarthy, op. cit., pp. 66f.

42. McCarthy, ibid., pp. 285f.

43. Ibid., p. 286. For Habermas's use of Kohlberg and Piaget, among others, in the articulation of nonidentity in the social formation of ego-identity, cf. ibid., pp. 31–57.

44. Buck-Morss, op. cit., p. 189.

45. Horkheimer, *Critical Theory,* p. v.

46. Habermas, *Protestbewegung und Hochschulreform* (Frankfurt: Suhrkamp, 1969); for translations of some of this material, cf. *Toward a Rational Society,* pp. 1–49.

47. Cf. Aronowitz's "Introduction" to the American translation of Horkheimer's *Critical Theory,* pp. xi–xxi.

48. Cf. *Essential Frankfurt School Reader,* pp. 1–25, 71–94; and Leszek Kolakowski, *Main Currents of Marxism,* vol. 3, *The Breakdown,* trans. P. Falla (Oxford: Clarendon Press, 1978), pp. 341–420.

49. Paul Baran and Paul Sweezy, *Monopoly Capital* (New York: Monthly Review Press, 1966); Harry Braverman, *Labor and Monopoly Capital* (New York: Monthly Review Press, 1974); Marc Linder with Julius Sensat, *Anti-Samuelson* (New York: Urizen Books, 1977).

50. Karl Marx, *Capital* (New York: International Publishers, 1967), vol. 3, p. 250.

51. Sensat, op. cit., pp. 79–124.

52. Schroyer, op. cit., pp. 224–53; Schroyer is drawing upon Martin Sklar's analysis of disaccumulation in late capitalism.

53. Schroyer, ibid., p. 240.

54. Cf. McMurtry, op. cit., pp. 174–87; Marcuse, *Soviet Socialism,* pp. 85–103; and J. Wilczynski, *The Economics of Socialism,* 3 ed. (London: George Allen and Unwin, 1977).

55. Schroyer, op. cit., pp. 249f.; on the need to understand economic theory in the concrete historical contexts in which it arose, cf. Adolf Lowe, *On Economic Knowledge* (New York: Harper & Row, 1965).

56. Schroyer, op. cit., p. 250.

57. Cf. Bernard Lonergan, *Insight: A Study of Human Understanding* (New York: Harper & Row, 1978, paperback ed.), pp. 207–44, 595–633. Lonergan has elaborated a critical macroeconomics which puts the accumulation and disaccumulation phases into an explanatory framework, cf. his *An Essay in Circulation Analysis* (Boston: Boston College, 1978, n.p.).

58. Cf. Joseph O'Malley, "Marx, Marxism and Method," in S. Avineri, *The Varieties of Marxism,* pp. 1–50; Schroyer, op. cit., pp. 171–223; M. Horkheimer and T. Adorno, *Aspects of Sociology,* trans. John Viertel (Boston: Beacon Press, 1972). On the need to correct Marx, cf. Dietrich Böhler, *Metakritik der Marxschen Ideologiekritik* (Frankfurt: Suhrkamp, 1971).

59. Cf. Schroyer, op. cit., pp. 250ff.

60. Cf. Samuel Bowles and Herbert Gintis, *Schooling in Capitalist America: Educational Reform and the Contradictions of Economic Life* (New York: Basic Books, 1976); Daniel Bell, *The Cultural Contradictions of Capitalism* (New York: Basic Books, 1976); David Smith, *Who Rules the Universities?* (New York: Monthly Review, 1974).

61. Cf. Schroyer, op. cit., pp. 250–53; G. Radnitzky, *Contemporary Schools of Metascience* (Göteborg: Akademiförlaget, 1970).

62. Richard Bernstein, *Praxis and Action* (Philadelphia: University of Pennsylvania Press, 1971); *The Restructuring of Social and Political Theory.*

63. Cf. writings of Alvin Gouldner in n. 3 and 23 above.

64. Lasch, *Haven in a Heartless World: The Family Besieged* (New York: Basic Books, 1977) and his *The Culture of Narcissism* (New York: W. W. Norton and Co., 1978).

65. Cf. M. Lamb, *History, Method and Theology,* pp. 357–456; also his "The Production Process and Exponential Growth," in F. Lawrence (ed.), *Lonergan Workshop* (Missoula: Scholar's Press, 1978), pp. 257–307.

66. Cf. Helmut Peukert, *Wissenschaftstheorie-Handlungstheorie-Fundamentale Theologie* (Frankfurt: Suhrkamp, 1978); on the dialectical analysis still needed in this compare Bernstein, *Praxis and Ac-*

*tion*, pp. 165–229, with George Novack, *Pragmatism versus Marxism* (New York: Pathfinder Press, 1975).

67. Cf. Karl Marx and Friedrich Engels, *On Religion*, ed. Reinhold Niebuhr (New York: Schocken Books, 1964), pp. 41ff. On sacralism and secularism, cf. H. Bartsch (ed.), *Probleme der Entsakralisierung* (Mainz: Grünewald, 1970); Karl Derksen (ed.), *Les deux visages de la théologie de la sécularisation* (Tournai: Casterman, 1970), and M. Lamb, "The Production Process and Exponential Growth," pp. 265–84.

68. Cf. Marcel Xhaufflaire, *Feuerbach et la théologie de la sécularisation* (Paris: Editions du Cerf, 1970), pp. 307–86. H. Peukert, op. cit., pp. 300–55.

69. Cf. S. Torres and J. Eagleson (eds.), *Theology in the Americas* (New York: Orbis Books, 1976); Robert McAfee Brown, *Theology in a New Key* (Philadelphia: Westminster Press, 1978); Alfred Hennelly, *Theologies in Conflict* (New York: Orbis Press, 1979).

70. Cf. Johann B. Metz, *Faith in History and Society*.

71. Cf. Gregory Baum, *Religion and Alienation* (New York: Paulist Press, 1975); H. Peukert, *Wissenschaftstheorie-Handlungstheorie-Fundamentale Theologie;* M. Lamb, *History, Method and Theology;* Russell B. Norris, *God, Marx and the Future* (Philadelphia: Fortress Press, 1974). On the Christian-Marxist dialogue, cf. Peter Hebblethwaite, *The Christian-Marxist Dialogue* (New York: Paulist Press, 1977); Ernst Bloch, *Atheism in Christianity*, trans. J. Swann (New York: Herder and Herder, 1972); the essays in *Study Encounter*, 4/1 (1968); M. Machoveč, *A Marxist Looks at Jesus* (Philadelphia: Fortress Press, 1976); Anthony Cuschieri, "The Christian-Marxist Encounter," in *Cross Currents* 27/3 (1977): 279–97; Johann B. Metz (ed.), *Christianity and Socialism* (New York: Seabury Press, 1977); N. Piediscalzi and R. Thobaben (eds.), *From Hope to Liberation* (Philadelphia: Fortress Press, 1974).

72. Cf. Norman Gottwald, *The Tribes of Yahweh* (New York: Orbis Books, 1979); L. John Topel, *The Way to Peace: Liberation Through the Bible* (New York: Orbis Books, 1979); Ben F. Meyer, *The Aims of Jesus* (London: SCM Press, 1979); also chap. 4 below and references given there.

73. Cf. references to Metz and Peukert in n. 70 and 71 above; also R. Siebert, "Peukert's New Critical Theology," in *The Ecumenist* 16/4:52–58 and 16/5:78–80.

74. Cf. references in n. 69 and 71 above; also G. Baum, *The Social Imperative* (New York: Paulist Press, 1979).

# Chapter 3

# The Relationship between Theory and Praxis in Contemporary Christian Theologies

**T**he relationship of theory and praxis goes right to the core of the entire philosophical enterprise; it involves the relations of consciousness to being, of subject to object, of idea to reality, of word to deed, of meaning to history.[1] Similarly in theology, this relationship goes beyond a discussion of contemplative or active ways of life to raise such fundamental issues as the relations of faith to love, of church to world, of orthodoxy to orthopraxy, of salvation to liberation, of religion to political concerns, of historical and systematic to moral and pastoral theology. Even an adequate bibliography of the theory-praxis relationship in contemporary Christian theologies would extend far beyond the limits of the present study.

I shall attempt, therefore, to provide a framework of models or types within which to situate the main differences in the relationships of theory and praxis operative in contemporary Christian theologies.[2] Such an approach is open to the danger of taxonomic superficiality, especially when it is constrained by the demands of brevity in areas so extensive in scope and rich in nuance. Nonetheless, as H. Richard Niebuhr reminds us, it is possible to begin the task of bringing some order into this multiplicity if we can discern types dependent upon "the nature of the problem itself and the meanings of its terms."[3] The first section will sketch certain main issues in the nature of the problem and how the typology elaborates various contexts of usage defining the meanings of the terms *theory* and *praxis* in theologies. Each of the subsequent sections will outline chief characteristics of the types and constitutive elements of the theologies exemplifying those types.

## The Nature of the Problem

Philosophical and theological reflections on the relations between theory and praxis have, from their origin down to the present, involved at least three recurrent issues.

First, there is what might be termed the reflex character of the relationship. Generically, there is no cognition which is not an action, nor any human action which is not in some manner cognitive. Although the sources of theory and praxis are within human subjects, they have different orientations. Theory regards objective knowledge as the formulation and verification of intelligibilities; it primarily regards possible, probable, or certain constructs of reality. Through theory we seek the objective; theorizing aims at bypassing subjectivity by opening up objective spheres of reality, of what is possibly, probably, or certainly so. Theory represents the orientation of the subject-toward-objectivity. Praxis regards human action as what we actually do, and probably or possibly can do. Minimally, it could be a mere technical or mechanical repetition of movements, assembly-line routines with slight subjective engagement. More adequately, praxis is involvement and commitment; by our actions we become who we are. It is intersubjective; through praxis we live in a world with others as authentic or inauthentic subjects. Praxis represents the orientation of the subject-toward-subjectivity.[4] The diversity of orientation between theory and praxis raises the issue of how they are reflexly interrelated.

A second recurrent issue transposes the reflex character of the relation into a quest for norms of truth and of genuine human living. Despite the welter of often conflicting answers to the normativity questions, I would argue that there are three dominant tendencies in approaching the issue of norms. A *classical* tendency relates the norms to absolute, necessary reality or ideality; here the reflex character gives primacy to theory, as in Aristotle's notion of theoretic science governed by the metaphysical ideal of necessary first principles, or in Hegel's sublation of praxis by theory as the absolute idea.[5] An *empirical* tendency measures the norms according to verifiability or falsifiability within material reality as somehow publicly observable; here the reflex character acknowledges theory as intrinsically hypothetical, but tends to identify praxis with the manipulative techniques of modern natural scientific methods.[6] A *critical* tendency relates the norms to structural dynamics of individual and/or collective human performance; here the reflex character accords a primacy to praxis, while there are disputes about how praxis (including the praxis of theorizing) is to be understood critically, or which dynamics of human performance are foundationally normative.[7]

A third recurrent issue is a continued implication of religious categories. The theory-praxis discussion takes a positive or negative stance vis-à-vis religion whenever it turns to its own presuppositions.[8] Here too, one might delineate three tendencies. One tendency would so stress the religious dimension of theory-praxis, as in the theocratic orientation of classical cultures, that an undifferentiated *sacralized* context would prevail—a tendency illustrated in the cultural sacralizations of the Greco-Roman and medieval civilizations.[9] In reaction to the heteronomy resulting from the undifferentiation of secular and sacral, the emergence of empirical and critical normativity can so stress the autonomy of theory-praxis that any relation to theonomy is rejected as alienating—as illustrated in the undifferentiated *secularism* of much modern thought and practice.[10] Philosophers and theologians struggling with theory-praxis relations today are, in differing ways, articulating alternatives to sacralism and secularism. The main thrust is, as Bernard Lonergan and Eric Voegelin remind us, a critical differentiation of consciousness and social life proportionate to the exigencies of truly critical theory and genuinely liberating praxis, of knowing the truth through doing the truth, which would tend toward a differentiated *sacred-secular* context.[11]

These three recurrent issues coalesce today in a quest for the foundations of theory and praxis grounding a proper complementarity between the gospel imperatives of enlightening and converting, between incarnation and eschatology, between Christian universalism and the particularity of church traditions, between the tasks of interpreting and changing the world, between judgments of fact and judgments of value, between empirical methods of research and critical methods of dialectics. If Hegel's "consciousness determines social life" is not to end in the escapism of romantic utopianism, and if Marx's "social life determines consciousness" is not to end in the triumph of biased facticity, then differentiation of consciousness mediated in social life is a present imperative for theology, as well as the other human sciences and scholarly disciplines.

Insofar as the three recurrent issues explicate what Niebuhr calls "the nature of the problem," then a survey attentive to those issues can begin to thematize various models or types: how they handle the reflex character of theory-praxis; where they situate the norm; how theory and praxis relate to the Christian religion. Such models or types are disclosive of what Niebuhr calls "the meaning of the terms," not by offering generic definitions and then applying in the models specific differences but by disclosing various *contexts of usage* which define the meaning of the terms relative to how they are used and the contexts within which their users operate. Such a procedure is intrinsically open and ongoing as a method of *dialectical* analysis, the goal of which is to spell out all the relevant concrete, dynamic, and contradictory elements in the affinities and oppositions of the usage.[12] The present typology is concerned with how theologians relate the categories of theory and praxis to the Christian religion, and how that relating affects (and is affected by) their understanding of the reflex character and the normativity of theory-praxis. Such an approach is open to, indeed demands, further inquiry into the usage and users in terms of their ongoing psychological, social, political, and cultural contexts.[13] In the measure that I succeed in explicating the dialectical relations among the three recurrent issues, this study will provide a framework for surveying those further inquiries.[14]

The following types are structured according to how their usage of theory-praxis, with the three recurrent issues mentioned, exhibits what I shall term relations of primacy or correlations. The relations of primacy involve an either/or approach to whether or not Christianity is intrinsically or extrinsically determined by theory or praxis.[15] The primacy of theory type maintains that religion and theory are intrinsically related, while both have only an extrinsic relation to praxis. The primacy of praxis type envisions religion and praxis as intrinsically related, while theory remains more or less extrinsic. The primacy of faith-love type insists that genuine Christianity is only extrinsically related to theory-praxis, is always nonidentical with them. The final two types seek to sublate the relational primacy models by developing what I term a both/and stance of critical correlation.[16] Thus the critical theoretic correlation type emphasizes a theoretic mediation between Christianity and the categories of theory-praxis. The critical praxis correlation type seeks to articulate a praxis-grounded mediation.

## Five Models of Theory-Praxis

*The Primacy of Theory*

This type corresponds to David Tracy's orthodox model, where the self-referent "is to a believer in a specific church tradition and the object-referent is to a (usually systematic) understanding of those beliefs."[17] In terms of the theory-praxis relation, this type has influenced contemporary theologies especially by its heavy dependence upon Aristotelian and scholastic thought forms. The object-referent is an understanding of the faith within what Lonergan calls a classical cultural matrix, or Karl Rahner a traditional homogenous culture.[18] The designation "orthodox" is misleading. Theological "orthodoxy" was appropriated by Catholic and Protestant scholasticism at a time when the authority of classical culture and society was challenged by the beginnings of modern science and historical scholarship, by a radical humanism and an incipient industrialization. The reaction of Catholic scholastic theology was to refuse to differentiate the gospel message from its cultural systematic understanding and to retreat into a theoretical orthodoxy. In so doing, it solidified the replacement of the questioning attitude of the medieval *summae* with a dogmatic thesis theology dedicated to certainty and various forms of logical deductivism.[19]

The internal relation between Christianity and theory was assured by the medieval shift toward theory through the assimilation of an Aristotelian *Begrifflichkeit*. Theology, the object of which was God himself and all things related to him, was both speculative and practical science. However, as Aquinas noted, it was more speculative than practical since it dealt more with God than with human acts, and only with the latter as oriented to the *perfect knowledge* of God in eternal beatitude. *Theoria* was supreme as the knowledge of necessary and eternal truths or first principles.[20] This transposition of Aristotle did not include his distinctions between *praxis*, as the acts of citizens and statesmen who identified the good with honor, and *poiesis* concerned with the production of material objects. Thus praxis was variously rendered by *actio* and *factio*; and the doctrine of creation represented God, as infinite intelligence, as the *Artifex Mundi*. In the fourteenth century, Duns Scotus pushed this even further by acknowledging God as the "doable knowable," i.e., "the object of knowledge which may be reached by a doing which is true *praxis*."[21] This gave a more prominent place in theology to religious charity as the way to salvation through authentic practice. A decadent scholasticism, however, buried those insights in a rigorous logicism.

There are two contemporary variants which draw upon this primacy of theory type. The first simply transposes classicist categories, usually deformed beyond recognition, into theology. T. Howland Sanks has studied the doctrine of the magisterium taught by the Gregorian University theologians between Vatican I and Vatican II.[22] His study, and Roman Catholic manuals of theology in general, indicate how the reflex character of theory-praxis is minimalized by the conceptualistic logicism of theory. Man's innate ability to know eternal and necessary truths was translated by neoscholasticism into a primacy of logic. Faith is the response to supernaturally revealed truths which are "deposited" in the church, whose task it is to guard, defend, and propagate them. The normativity of theology is found in the teaching authority of the church as a hierarchically structured magisterium. Development of doctrine is accounted for by the application of logic (virtual predication, etc.) to the deposit. Moral and pastoral theology are basically prudential applications of dogmatic theory and hierarchical authority, which latter remains essentially the same despite variations in prudential applications. Ecclesial institutional structure is hierarchical on the model of a pure, rather than constitutional, monarchy. The untimely message of the gospel seems identified with being-out-of-date.[23]

The second variant of the primacy of theory can be found in the more sophisticated Thomism of theologians such as Charles Journet and Garrigou-Lagrange, and as preeminently articulated by Jacques Maritain. Although not a "professional" theologian but a Christian philosopher, Maritain is by far the best representative of this primacy of theory type. His *Degrees of Knowledge* is its finest expression, and the manifold applications range throughout his other writings. He accepts the Aristotelian norm for scientific knowledge as necessary "irrefragable" intelligibility; he contrasts the intelligible universes (the objects of scientific and sapiential knowledge) and the "contingent," irreversible flux of the universe of existence. "Science," he writes, as "knowledge in the strict sense of the word, considers only the intelligible necessities immersed in the reality of this world of existence."[24] He adopts Aquinas's three degrees of abstraction to move from infrascientific experience, through physics and the natural sciences and mathematics, to natural philosophy and metaphysical science or wisdom.

We are reminded that "it would be foolish to imagine that this universe (of contingent existence) could be completely reclaimed by human science" since its contingencies are "not as such the objects of science in the strict sense."[25] Maritain then distinguishes three wisdoms: metaphysical wisdom (knowledge of first principles), theological wisdom (knowledge of revealed truths), and infused mystical knowledge (contemplative connatural knowledge).[26] The ascent to being is complemented by a descent to action as one moves from pure speculation (knowledge for its own sake) to speculatively practical knowledge (moral theology and moral philosophy) which directs action from afar, through practically practical knowledge (practical moral sciences) which directs action from nearby, to prudence which directs action immediately.[27] The practice of fraternal charity is cathartic, purifying the human person for the higher, agapic wisdom of union with God.

Similar to Aristotle, Maritain relates this framework to the life of praxis or the temporal order of political and social institutions. In his *Integral Humanism* he readily admits that the sacralization of the temporal order in the Holy Roman Empire is definitively past. Yet there is a present imperative to work for "the historical ideal of a new Christendom," to "build up an Empire for Christ" wherein the church would continue to be the "crucified kingdom of God."[28] This new Christendom would, through the principles of analogy and a prudential application of Thomistic "common good" doctrine, foster an organic democracy and pluralism. The new Christendom would be the work of the Catholic laity, and Catholic action directed by a *théologie politique* (*not* a German *politische Theologie*) maintaining the distinction between the sacral and the secular, while advocating the directive influence of the sacral on the secular. Amid the vicissitudes of history, the church maintains her holy, spiritual, and doctrinal identity.[29]

The reflex character of this type, then, does not see the ontological structure of reality, or being, intrinsically changed by praxis. The latter is a propaedeutic for us to ascend to supracontingent wisdom. Normativity is in the eternal and necessary, not in the flux of the universe of existence. Christian faith and love are intrinsically related to theory as the highest form of wisdom. The sacred and the secular are "distinguished to be united" in a new Christendom.

### The Primacy of Praxis

This type articulates an internal relation between Christianity and praxis, whereas theory is understood primarily as a more or less extrinsic reflection on that praxis. Three main variants of this type might be distinguished according to whether praxis is understood as cultural-historical activity, liberal sociopolitical reform activity, or radical Marxist revolutionary praxis respectively. These variants have in common a more or less thorough rejection of classical-traditionalist metaphysics. Theory is not given a necessary domain of eternal truths but is seen as no more

than ever revisable approximations to the flux of contingent
events in history. Theological theory as doctrines or dogmas does
not provide normativity, but is accorded a secondary, external
relation to praxis. Theology as theory may be more or less helpful but not intrinsically determinative of praxis. Its reflex character consists in "the explicit commitment of the Christian theologian to the basic cognitive claims and ethical values" of either
modern secular or contemporary secular periods.[30]

This type of theory-praxis relationship, then, includes both
the liberal and radical models expounded by David Tracy. The
first two variants are constituted by the liberal horizon, the self-
referent of which is the theologian's own "consciousness as committed to the basic values of modernity," and the object-
referent is principally "the Christian tradition (usually the tradition of one's own church) as reformulated in accordance with
such modern commitments and critiques."[31] The third variant is
even more radical than Tracy's radical model insofar as it criticizes the postmodern secular affirmation and theistic negation in
the death-of-God theologians for being a form of crypto-reli-
gious ideology in a one-dimensional society.[32]

The cultural-historical primacy of praxis has its roots both in
Luther's repudiation of speculative theology and in the Enlightenment's rejection of metaphysics in favor of empirical-critical
studies of nature and history. Schleiermacher laid the ground-
work for this type by distinguishing religious experience from
metaphysics and morals; by making historical theology ground
philosophical theology and verify practical theology as dedicated to the needs of the Christian church in its pastoral practice. The eternal and infinite is not found in theoretical constructs but in the emotive-intuitive experience of believers. The
church is a locus of freedom in contrast to the state as repre-
senting heteronomous authority.[33] Troeltsch corrected the con-
fessionalism of Schleiermacher and carried the historicity of theology further by revealing the conflicting institutional contexts
of religious practice (ideal types of church and sect). His *theological* dependence on the psychological need for religious faith,
along with his radical acceptance of historical-critical methods
and his identification of the goal of the Kingdom of God with

human purposefulness—all these indicate a fundamental acceptance of modern historical secularity.[34]

Contemporary forms of this primacy of cultural-historical experience in the theological articulation of faith embrace such
diverse works as Leslie Dewart's *The Future of Belief* and *The
Foundations of Belief,* Gabriel Moran's *The Present Revelation,*
Paul Van Buren's *The Secular Meaning of the Gospel,* and Eu-
gene Fontinell's "Religious Truth in a Relational and Processive
World."[35] The dehellenization of doctrine, its deontologizing,
opens theology to reflect upon revelation as a present ongoing
event. Knowledge is elusive. The general tenor of these writings
in regard to religious truth is that it

> consists not in correspondence with an outside reality but
> in enabling one to participate more fully in the ongoing
> processive reality with which man is continuous. Creeds
> and dogmas, therefore, are not to be assessed in terms of
> the knowledge about God they are thought to convey,
> but in terms of their ability to help man move beyond the
> relatively inadequate situation in which he finds himself
> and to expand his life within the human community.[36]

Perhaps the most cogent expression of this form of theology is
the position of Van A. Harvey. The "soft perspectivism," which
allows theology to overcome the antinomy between the morality
of a scientific culture and the morality of a Christian believer, is
contrasted with the tendency to exclusivity or "hard perspectivism" on the part of H. Richard Niebuhr. The moral-practical
and historical dimensions of every perspective mean that they
cannot be abstractly described; they are rather "field-encom-
passing affairs" involving symbol, myth, image. Revelation
is not the imparting of truths but the event of reconciliation.
There is, strictly speaking, no *exclusive* Christian perspective
but an inclusive one. It has a disclosive capacity theologians
must carefully articulate, not by proof, but by remaining
faithful to the inclusive significance of its symbols and historical destiny; they must creatively relate those symbols to
the differing social, historical, and cultural communities of
believers.[37]

A second variant of the primacy of praxis type articulates the reflex character of the theory-praxis relation and the normativity in terms of liberal sociopolitical action. Its roots are in the Kantian relation of religion to morality, and the Ritschlian distinction between the speculative judgments of science and the value judgment of religion. Eschewing any form of dogmatism and Hellenic speculation in theology, it sought to uncover the central significance of Christian faith in God-as-love; revelation did not communicate truths to be believed so much as ideals by which people could live.[38] This found a popular presentation and concrete application in the Social Gospel movement in America, with its demands for a new theology capable of expressing the supposedly pristine message of Jesus and the reformers.[39]

A prominent example of this form of theologizing can be found in the secular city debates prompted by Harvey Cox. The repudiation of metaphysical categories is to reveal the true import of the good news: "Theology is a living enterprise. The Gospel does not call man to return to a previous stage of his development. It does not summon man back to dependency, awe and religionism. Rather it is a call to imaginative urbanity and mature secularity."[40] In criticizing the existentialist variants of non-metaphysical theology, orthodox models, and the linguistic approach of Van Buren, Cox called for a recognition of an urbane political normativity for theology:

> We have already suggested that God comes to us today in events of social change, in what theologians have often called *history*, what we call *politics*. But events of social change need not mean upheavals and revolutions. The events of everyday life are also events of social change. The smallest unit of society is two, and the relationship between two people never remains just the same. God meets us there, too. He meets us not just in the freedom revolution in America, but also in a client, a customer, a patient, a co-worker.[41]

In later writings Cox corrected his too enthusiastic approval of technical man and urbane polity.

The final variant of the primacy of praxis rejects not only the primacy of theory type but also both previous forms of this type. As represented in the Criticial Catholicism movement, theologians such as Frans v.d. Oudenrijn, Marcel Xhaufflaire, and Karl Derksen criticize both the secularization and death-of-God theologies for not understanding praxis radically enough. They draw upon Marx's critique of Hegel and Feuerbach in order to elucidate what they consider to be the ideology underpinning these attempts at relating the gospel to modern or contemporary society.[42] In their view only a theology which submits to the normativity of Marx's notion of praxis has any chance of authentically articulating a criticism both of contemporary society as well as all past and present theologies. They would see Thomas Altizer's questioning acceptance of Eric Voegelin's *The Ecumenic Age* as a demonstration of the ideological ambiguity of the death-of-God theologies as mere extensions of a cultural-historical notion of praxis.[43] With Marx, Oudenrijn tends to see past and present theology as "bad theory." Unlike philosophical theory, which could be sublated by revolutionary praxis, theology can only be negated as the quintessential alienation of man in capitalist society.[44] Critical theology can only be a critique of theology—not from the perspective of some overarching theoretical or practical system, nor in the name of the abstract species-being of humankind, but through a careful analysis of the concrete structures of domination in church and society. As Charles Davis commented on this position:

> History is basically the history of men's productive activities and the social relationships resulting from them. It is an error to think that religion was the dominant factor determining society in the past, and it is equally erroneous to suppose that the replacement of religion by some other form of theoretical thought is going to transform society in the future. . . . The *praxis* of Christians, like all *praxis*, demands a critical analysis of present society, intended to uncover the contradictions latent within it. These contradictions, if Christianity is more than ideology, will occur where Christians with their faith and hope are situated in an objective conflict with the social order. Conscious Christian *praxis* is the actualization of the conflict thus uncovered.[45]

These theologians, therefore, offer no assurance that Marx was not right when he claimed that Christianity offered only alienating theoretical salvation. That issue will only be resolved through the dialectical participation of Christians in changing their church and the world.[46]

These primacy of praxis types agree in rejecting classical metaphysics. If Christianity is to be faithful to its task, it must be intrinsically involved in historical, cultural, political, social and/or revolutionary praxis. Doctrinal theory is at best extrinsic and secondary. The reflex character of theory-praxis tends toward a reduction of theory to reflection on praxis as variously understood. The normativity tends toward an *identification* of Christianity with modern, secular (liberal or Marxist) processes. What promotes the identification is good; what hinders it is wrong, such as the identification of Christianity with classical cultural practices in the primacy of theory types.

### The Primacy of Faith-Love

This type emphasizes the nonidentity of Christian faith-love vis-à-vis theory-praxis. It corresponds to Tracy's neoorthodox model where the self-referent of the theologian is a dialectical appropriation of the basic attitudes of Christian faith, trust, and agapic love, while the object-referent is "the wholly other God of Jesus Christ."[47] In the light of theory-praxis, however, I would argue that theologians who exemplify more the mediational aspects of transcendence (such as Brunner, Bultmann, Tillich, the Niebuhrs, and Rahner) cannot be adequately treated under the primacy of faith-love type.

The prototype of faith's nonidentity relation to human theory-praxis is Karl Barth, especially in his early period. God is not the object of theology but its subject. He encounters humankind in Jesus Christ, the Word of God, as the concrete center and ground of all reality. Theology is possible only as obedience to that Word. As the debate between Barth and H. Scholz concerning the scientific character of theology indicated, Barth would not concede any theoretical norms for theology that were not intrinsic to faith.[48]

Theology, if it is to remain faithful to God's Word in faith, must manifest the crisis of judgment and grace, of condemnation and justification. The only criterion for the scientific character of theology is its *Sachgemässheit* relative to the Word.[49] A charge of theological fideism would be a compliment to Barth.

In Catholic theology the work of Hans Urs von Balthasar stresses a similar nonidentity between Christianity and theory-praxis. He criticizes the cosmological categories of scholasticism and Enlightenment natural religion, as well as the anthropological methods of transcendental Thomism and existentialist theologies.

> The criterion of genuine Christianity can be neither religious philosophy nor human existence. In philosophy man discovers what he can know of the depths of being, while in existence he brings what he can of these to life in himself. Christianity is destroyed if it lets itself be reduced to transcendental presuppositions of a man's self-understanding whether in thought or in life, in knowledge or in action.[50]

He seeks to avoid the extremes of extrinsicism and immanentism by adverting to what he calls "the third way of love." The gift character and "miracle" of an Other encountered in love, along with the aesthetic experience of unpredictable beauty, converge in von Balthasar's massive *Herrlichkeit* to explore the historical configurations of the Christian conversion encounter with the revealing Lord. The reality of God overpowers the shadows of this world, with all its efforts at theory or praxis.[51] If some indicate that von Balthasar has not yet adequately accounted for the paradox of his concern for aesthetic style in the very articulation of the shock quality of God's revelation, he would see that as the *coincidentia oppositorum* constitutive of the Christ-event, and of any truly Christian theology.[52] The "opposites" are not as radical as Barth's inasmuch as von Balthasar adopts a more patristic and monastic perspective on mysticism and spirituality. The central imperative of a genuine theology today must be a recovery of sanctity.[53]

As Barth's monumental *Church Dogmatics* and von Balthasar's *Herrlichkeit*—along with their extensive other writings—indicate, the nonidentity of Christian faith-love with human theory is still very much a *relational* nonidentity. Here the reflex character of the theory-praxis relation is, perhaps, best understood as a sophisticated theological parallel to Kierkegaard's paradoxical mode of communicating the contradictions and resolutions of human interiority.[54] The normativity is not "empirically" available (in the sense of critically provable by appeal to external data) but is rooted in the *decision* of Christian faith-love responding to the Word of God. The normativity, then, is radically gift and grace in a nonidentical relation to human experience.[55]

This nonidentity is also *relational* to praxis, as Barth's confrontation with "German Christians" indicates. Indeed, in Kierkegaard's usage, it is foundational for praxis, as Richard J. Bernstein has shown.[56] Another example of this could be found in the life and writings of Thomas Merton, who *paradoxically* as a contemplative monk confronted contemporary society with social and political judgment.[57] The *Hartford Appeal* presents, in my opinion, another variant of this nonidentity relation of Christian faith-love to theory and praxis. *Against the World for the World* is an apt paradoxical description of its call to halt any radical immanentizing of the Christian faith.[58]

In summary, the primacy of faith-love type locates the reflex character of theory-praxis in a supernaturalist paradoxical relation with the nonidentity of Christian revelation. Likewise, the question of normativity is approached within this nonidentical, paradoxical perspective: only God is normative in his revelation. The pentecostalist experience of the Spirit, or the mystic's dark night, or unconditional obedience to the Word—these are the touchstones of truth and life. The tendencies of the first two types are criticized for identifying Christianity with either classical or modern cultural matrices.

### Critical Theoretic Correlations

This type of reflection on the theory-praxis relationship seeks to establish a critical theoretic correlation between Christian tradition and the exigencies of theory and praxis. It basically accepts the affirmation of nonidentity elaborated in the previous type, but it criticizes the supernaturalist paradoxical mediation of that type. Indeed, theologians operating within this type or model maintain that the nonidentity or extrinsic relationship of Christian revelation vis-à-vis theory and praxis is not incompatible with the identity or intrinsic relations articulated in the first two types. They insist, however, that this correlation critically alters any exclusivity claims, which would absolutize the contingent, in any of the three previous types (whether that occurs regarding church, literal meaning of scripture, historical Jesus, metaphysics of classicism, modern secularity, or Marxist revolution). Perhaps, if a teutonicism is permitted, the theologians of the present type seek through their correlations to articulate a union of identity and nonidentity between Christianity and the categories of theory-praxis. That union is constituted, however, by critical theoretic correlations rather than the critical praxis correlations of the fifth type.

I would suggest that this type of theologically mediating the theory-praxis relation includes the mediational theologians sometimes designated as neoorthodox (especially Bultmann, Tillich, the Niebuhrs, Rahner), the universal-historical approach of Pannenberg, and the revisionist program of Tracy. A common characteristic of these theologians is an uncommon concern to articulate the theoretical issues confronting theology in a postmodern world. In terms of Tracy's models, this type corresponds both with his description of the revisionist theologian's horizon, and with those aspects of the neoorthodox horizon which indicate "the more radical model of the human being of authentic Christian faith."[59]

The mediational theologians tend to envisage the union-in-difference between theory and praxis within Christian theology as primarily established through the elaboration of an ontology which would do justice to both immanence and transcendence, to both the sociohistorical and the existential demands of Christian faith and practice.

Thus Bultmann correlated the historical-critical methods with the existential demands of decision-in-faith by several creative adaptations from Hermann, the law-gospel distinction, and Heideggerian categories. The level of *Historie* was completely open to the exigencies of empirical and critical analysis—the advances of liberal theology in appropriating modern methods of science and scholarship would not be abandoned. Faith, however, belonged to the ontic level of decision as *Geschichte*, and the critical task of theology was to check the tendency of everyone, believers and nonbelievers alike, to collapse one level into the other. Mediating the two levels was the pastoral practice of a kerygma informed by the critical advances of theology.[60]

The earlier Tillich's concern with Christianity and socialism was transposed (many would say abandoned) in his later work. He sought critically to correlate Christianity and contemporary culture through an ontology of human finitude open to the question of God, capable of overcoming the dichotomies between heteronomous and autonomous reason through an appropriation of the theonomous dimensions of reason-as-question answered through Christian revelation. *Praxis,* as social and cultural acts directed toward the just and the good, and *theoria,* as the cognitive and aesthetic acts directed at the true and the beautiful, are both open to the ambiguities of self-creation (the subject-object split) which constitute scientific and ethical methods as questions for revelation:

> Practice resists theory, which it considers inferior to itself; it demands an activism which cuts off every theoretical investigation before it has come to its end. In practice one cannot do otherwise, for one must act before one has finished thinking. On the other hand, the infinite horizons of thinking cannot supply the basis for any concrete decision with certainty. Except in the technical realm where an existential decision is not involved, one must make decisions on the basis of limited or distorted or incomplete insights. Neither theory nor practice in isolation can solve the problem of their conflict with each other. Only a truth which is present in spite of the infinity of theoretical possibilities and only a good which is present in spite of the infinite risk implied in every action can overcome the disruption between the grasping and the shaping functions of reason. The quest for such a truth and such a good is the quest for revelation.[61]

This correlation structure should not be interpreted as just another variant of Barth's supernatural paradox. Tillich's criticisms

of Barth and his own efforts at explicating the reasonable basis
for paradoxical language, as well as his notion of autonomy in
theonomy, preclude this.[62]

Karl Rahner's transcendental anthropology sought to ground a
critical correlation between the ontological structures of human
existence and the interpretation of ecclesial doctrines. He employed that philosophical-theological correlation to disclose the
many possibilities of concrete change needed within both the
church's teaching and its practice. Rahner effectively criticized
the ideal of a "new Christendom" or any form of church practice or teaching which would collapse the transcendental into
the categorical, that would abolish the nonidentity (and the
freedom and pluralism it preserves) in the name of a monolithic
identity. His transcendental anthropology enabled Rahner to
correlate the mysterious transcendence of God with the immanence of historical man as intrinsically a hearer of the Word.
Within this perspective, he sketches the outlines of a formal existential ethic and elaborates the social-critical function of the
church.[63]

These mediational theologies exhibit the reflex character of
theory-praxis as a reflection on the ontological structures common to human existence and Christian revelation. The normativity question, therefore, is more open to a mutual interaction
between reason and faith.

The universal-historical perspective of Pannenberg criticizes
these characteristics of the mediational positions insofar as he
questions whether the transcendental-existential correlations in
theology "do not sufficiently secure the objective foundation of
faith."[64] He proposes, instead, to articulate the objective facticity of revelation within history understood as the whole of
history anticipated eschatologically in Christian faith. Thus,
there is no question of attempting to create some transcenden-
tal-ontological realm or level of reality impervious to historical-
critical methods. The horizon of the whole of history, the meaning of which will only be revealed at its end, both promotes the
intrinsic access of theology to the sciences and historical-critical
methods, while also emphasizing their hypothetical-tentative
results. The debates his *Revelation as History* provoked have led

Pannenberg to a more differentiated stance regarding subjectivity and objectivity. In his *Wissenschaftstheorie und Theologie* he admits that:

> The reality of God is co-given only in subjective anticipations of the totality of reality, in pro-jects toward the totality of meaning which are co-posited in every individual experience. These pro-jects are for their part historical, i.e., they remain exposed to the process of experience for their confirmation or rejection.[65]

Thus theology as the science of God is only possible as the science of religion; God is only indirectly revealed in history. Its difference from other religious studies consists in theology's questioning of religious traditions "as to how extensively their tradition documents a self-manifestation of divine reality."[66] Pannenberg goes on to show how this understanding of theology allows it to assimilate the many advances in the philosophy of science, how like philosophy and modern science it is faced with the correlation of the normative and the hypothetical, and also how the relation to life-praxis is intrinsic to theology.[67] He sees the special task of "practical theology" to articulate the theory-praxis relation in the light of ecclesial praxis.[68]

David Tracy's revisionist project closely parallels—and in many decisive ways advances—the position of Pannenberg. That the sources of theology are common human experience and Christian texts, that the method of investigating the former is phenomenological, and of the latter historical and hermeneutical—these aspects of the revisionist model parallel Pannenberg's closely. Pannenberg's realization (that a subject-oriented anticipation of totality is constitutive of theology) is advanced, in my opinion, by Tracy's use of a transcendental-metaphysical mode of reflection in determining the truth-status for theology.[69] Although Pannenberg might wince at the assertion that "there must be a necessary and a sufficient ground in our common experience" for the truth-claims of religion, his own articulation of the criteria for assessing the truth-claims would be decisively complemented by Tracy's explicitation of how the religious horizon grounds, and is implicit in, all dimensions of known historical experience, and how that is expressed in limit-language and the criteria of adequacy, appropriateness, and coherence.[70] Tracy's more recent work not only corrects his previous misinterpretations of political and liberation theologies but also acknowledges how, at least for the theologies of praxis, theory not only aims at praxis but is also grounded in praxis.[71] *The Analogical Imagination* creatively advances the discussion in *Blessed Rage for Order* by suggesting a complementarity between three theological disciplines, each mainly (but not exclusively) addressed to three distinct publics and motivated by three distinct transcendental orientations:

| | | |
|---|---|---|
| Foundational Theology | Academic Public | Truth (Metaphysics, Dialectics) |
| Systematic Theology | Ecclesial Public | Beauty (Poetics, Rhetoric) |
| Practical Theology | Social Public | Good (Ethics, Politics) |

Although Tracy does not advert to it, these are more differentiated, contemporary distinctions, analogous to those made by Varro, and analyzed by Saint Augustine, between natural, mythical, and civil theologies.[72] The brilliance of Tracy's analysis consists in its capacity to range phenomenologically over the many subjects elaborated by contemporary theologians, trying to correlate their many differences in ways that would disclose them as basically complementary. But, as his own discussion of the various Christian responses in the contemporary situation intimates, such a disclosive or phenomenological analysis may not be adequate to the tasks of concretely transforming the pervasive alienations and distortions operative in those theologies and running throughout the academic, ecclesial, and social publics.[73] The diverse interpretations of both the religious traditions and the contemporary situations do indeed admit of genetic and complementary correlations. *The Analogical Imagination* decisively moves beyond Pannenberg, and Tracy's own previous work, in understanding the limits of complementarity. Within practical theologies Tracy acknowledges how the interpretations and histories of the classics often confront us with contradictory responses to situations which demand, not complementarity, but the dialectics which call for theologians to take a stand critically in terms of intellectual, moral, and religious imperatives. The cries of the victims are heard in his descriptions of the present situation and of the responses of political and liberation theologies.

In this sense Tracy's latest work is transitional to the theologies of the next type. In one important methodological aspect, nevertheless, even it remains in a critical theoretic correlation. If I understand his complementary distinctions (not separations) between foundational, systematic, and practical theologies correctly, then he has not worked out how the theological positions he discusses *within* those distinctions might themselves call for dialectical differences rather than complementarity. Tracy admits that his efforts to distinguish their complementarity is within foundational theology.[74] Obviously the theologians who do liberation or political reflection argue rather persuasively that their practical theologies are foundational and systematic; they address not only society but also the academy and church. They would, then, challenge Tracy's understanding of foundational and systematic disciplines. To what extent are Tracy's distinctions unintentional ways of theoretically immunizing the disciplines of foundations and systematics against the claims of liberation and political theologies? This question will become ever more urgent as Tracy investigates the foundational import of the theologies of praxis. I suspect his analysis in *The Analogical Imagination* remains inadequate on this issue.

Acknowledging the many differences between these mediational theologians, I believe the critical correlations they offer are primarily theoretic unities of identity and nonidentity inasmuch as the reflex relationship of theory-praxis is *intrinsically open to* and therefore *in part constituted by* a nonidentity they variously name faith-decision, ultimate concern, openness to mystery, subjective anticipation of totality, primordial faith in the ultimate worth of our existence, or intensified encounter with classic religious events and texts. Normativity is determined by this theoretic (metaphysical, phenomenological, or ontologically hermeneutical) union of identity and nonidentity insofar as it enables them to avoid the tendencies toward the reductionist identities of the first two types, or toward the fideism of the third type.

### Critical Praxis Correlations

This type of theological reflection on the relationship of theory and praxis, as the previous type, seeks a critical union of identity and nonidentity between the categories of theory-praxis and Christianity. It differs from the previous type, however, inasmuch as the critical correlation is placed in praxis rather than in theory. The theoretical correlation of the previous type was primarily metaphysical in character, open to, yet not identical with, the empirical sciences and critical historical disciplines. Unlike classicist metaphysical theories, the theologians of the previous type, in different manners, insist that the *aim* or *goal* of theory is praxis (understood as action, whether as a personal, social, cultural, political, or religious phenomenon). The present theologians differ from them since, in one way or another, they claim that the union-in-difference between theory and praxis, i.e., its reflex character, means that praxis itself as action or performance grounds the activity of theorizing. *Praxis is not only the goal but also the foundation of theory.* This applies to any theorizing, including theology. The demands of theory for coherence and adequacy, for rigorous verification of truth-claims, are not minimized but intensified in this model. Those demands are intensified to the degree that theologians operating in this model or type recognize how those demands cannot be met by appeals to axioms, principles, paradigms, activist programs, faith commitments, or hermeneutical theories which neglect (or inadequately examine) the key questions involved in what really is done when we do theology.[75]

Unlike the first type with its primacy of theory, these theologians emphasize how metaphysics—especially classical metaphysics and, a fortiori, the decadent offsprings of classical metaphysics—can no longer serve as a foundational science of totality. For, as we saw in chapter two, theory is critical to the extent that it explicates its own foundations in transformative praxis. No theory *qua* theory can be critically self-grounding. No theory *qua* theory can sublate praxis, although praxis can sublate theory. Any and all theories making such claims of being self-grounded or of being able to sublate praxis—and Hegel's was certainly among the most genial and pretentious—are only setting themselves up for an inevitable fall.[76] Unlike the primacy of praxis types of theologizing, theologians in this model acknowledge the impossibility of finding a practical reason that is pure or innocent. The basic values of modernity have brought us too many victims whose cries unmask the pretended innocence of the many forms of secularist practical reason. As chapter one tried to show, we cannot justify human existence by simply identifying the gospel message with contemporary secular values or movements. Moreover, there is a tendency among theologians operating in the second type to reject religious traditions too easily. In doing this, however, they find it difficult to express their solidarity with the many past victims of history.[77]

Unlike the theologians of the third type, theologians committed to critical praxis correlations acknowledge how the revelation of values operative in the Jewish and Christian religious traditions, while transcending the claims of pure reason, are nonetheless symbolically constitutive of reason as yet to be realized in history and society. Take, for example, Lonergan's proposals in his *Method in Theology*. He frankly avows that he is a conservative Roman Catholic theologian, but his program for a new way of doing theology in terms of functional specialization could also be constitutive for any disciplines concerned with the human past and confronting the challenges of our ambiguous human future. "For transcendental method is the concrete and dynamic unfolding of human attentiveness, intelligence, reasonableness, and responsibility."[78] Another example would be the theological praxis of Johann B. Metz. Like Barth and von Balthasar, he insists upon the revealed truths and values of Judaeo-Christian eschatology and apocalyptic as expressive of the cries of the victims of history. But, unlike them, Metz has labored long in attempting to institutionalize a new way of doing theology at the proposed Graduate Theological Research Center at the University of Bielefeld. The whole thrust of this practical

project was to bring those values to bear upon a critical interdisciplinary collaboration between theology and the other sciences and scholarships. Just as Lonergan's program has yet to be
implemented in any academic faculty of religious studies or theology, so has Metz's program faced the intransigence of bureaucratic fears and doubts.[79]

Nor have these apparent "failures"—or that of Habermas at
the Max Planck Institute[80]—led these thinkers to abandon their
projects of instituting new ways of doing theology in an interdisciplinary context. Unlike theologians operating in the fourth
type of critical theoretic correlations, Lonergan and Metz remain convinced that it is not enough to produce learned tomes
on theology which leave the doing of theology within the present academic, ecclesial, and social contexts. As Lonergan has
remarked, the age of omnicompetent theologians has disap-
peared with the age of innocent theory.[81] Theory never was
really innocent, but after the modern horrors of our twentieth-
century history we can no longer responsibly continue doing
theology as if, for instance, a seminar on the holocaust could be
added to the old curriculum. Adapting Tracy's categories, I
would say that the self-referent of theologians in the critical
praxis correlation is their awareness that only authentic religious, moral, intellectual, psychic, and social forms of praxis can
ground an authentic doing of theology. The object-referent is
their varying efforts at thematizing new ways of doing theology
within an interdisciplinary collaboration which would promote
a critical praxis correlation that aims at academic, ecclesial, and
social transformations. These theologians acutely experience the
contradictions—not complementarity—between past and present theories, on the one hand, and the imperatives of authentically transformative praxis, on the other. They seek to articulate
those contradictions, thereby contributing to the liberation of
noetic praxis from the oppressive academic, ecclesial, and social
structures which both condition and are conditioned by those
theories.

These theologians challenge us with a call to change the way
we are doing theology. Their challenge goes to the very foundations of how we do theology today. They address their call to

conversion or change to the publics of the academy, the churches, and society at large. I shall illustrate very briefly how they do this in terms of Lonergan's call to method, Metz's political theology, and the various forms of liberation theologies.

Lonergan has effected a shift from theory to method which no longer appeals to a scholastic or a Kantian notion of transcendental reflection. Instead, he outlines a methodological control of meaning and value in terms of the critical experiment of self-appropriation, which verifies the related and recurrent operations of conscious intentionality in the praxis of that experiment.[82] From the foundations of that generalized empirical method, he has initiated a series of further determinations which relate those self-transformative and self-disclosive structures of freedom to the noetic praxis of the natural and human sciences, hermeneutical and historical scholarship, and a generalized method for the doing of theology. Since authentic praxis can never be solved by theories *qua* theories, Lonergan has articulated a *radical cognitive therapy* aimed at a basic liberation of human subjects through a heightening of their awareness whereby they appropriate the imperatives of human freedom as dynamic orientations to be attentive, to be intelligent, to be reasonable, to be responsible, and to be loving.[83]

Such an emancipatory method can ground, through its cognitive therapy, not only a reorientation of theology but also of the psychic and social appropriations of reality.[84] It positively sublates the appeal which Habermas makes to psychoanalytic therapy as a model for an emancipatory science of communicative interaction, as well as Habermas's more recent use of Kohlberg.[85] It transposes the ideal of an unlimited community of investigators, proposed by Habermas and Karl-Otto Apel, into the concrete context of personal and social self-correcting processes of learning and action within structures oriented toward the common good.[86] This involves, then, a fundamental commitment to interdisciplinary collaboration that is at once critical and creative. Lonergan's functional specialties in theology, like his cognitive therapy, are to be tested through the praxis of a wide-ranging interdisciplinary collaboration. It is through method so understood that theology is related to all other fields of human knowledge and action among the publics of academy, church, and society—not through mediations of philosophical theories per se. As I shall indicate in the next chapters, Lonergan addresses the ecclesial publics in his call for an articulation of orthopraxis as foundational to orthodoxy, just as he addresses the wider social publics in his efforts to articulate a critically functional macroeconomics.[87]

The political theologies emerging within Europe and North America are increasingly responsive to the global issues addressed by Third World liberation theologies.[88] As Metz, along with Trutz Rendtorff, has devoted much time to the Bielefeld project, so Helmut Peukert and other students of Metz have articulated the importance of theology entering into a critical academic collaboration with other sciences and scholarship. Anamnetic solidarity with the victims of history demands, among other elements, a noetic praxis which would transform the actual contexts of academies and universities. The alienating situations in advanced industrialized societies are intrinsically related with vast, complex institutions and processes of domination and control, extending throughout the so-called Third World. Hence the need for serious interdisciplinary collaboration in First World universities wherein theology would give voice to the victims.[89] Political theologians also address ecclesial publics with challenges to change. They elaborate theologies in which Christian symbols, narratives, and teachings are understood as expressing religious memories subversive of sacralist and secularist attitudes and policies. They call, as in Metz's *The Emergent Church*, for a transition from patriarchal-authoritarian, and from liberal-bourgeois, to liberating basic community forms of being church.[90] They address issues of broad social and cultural relevance, as in Soelle's analyses of literature, in Metz's exchanges with Rudolf Bahro, or in Gregory Baum's discussions of Canadian socialism. Feminist theologians within this model essay critical recoveries of traditions which, instead of either accepting or rejecting them wholesale, dialectically discern the negative and positive aspects of the traditions. This can be seen, for example, in Judith Plaskow's concern that Christian feminism not fall into an anti-Judaic bias, or in Elizabeth Fiorenza's work on early Christian feminism.[91]

Perhaps the strongest impact challenging the way theology is done today has come from the many types of liberation theologies. Rather than from an initial dialogue with either academic colleagues or church authorities, these theologies have emerged out of an ongoing dialogue and mutual learning process with the poor, oppressed, exploited races, classes, and sexes within histories and societies. Having heard and acted upon the cries of the many victims of "the way things are" in academy, church, and society, these theologies exercise a far more critical reflection upon the stands they adopt than theologians in the previous four types wish to concede. For their solidarity with the victims of sexism, racism, classism, militarism, and ecological pollution makes them especially attentive to, and critical of, the myriad forms of instrumental rationality which, as I pointed out in chapter two, are profoundly irrational and biased. The praxis or performance of these liberation theologies demonstrates how letting God be God as revealed in Jewish and Christian religious traditions simultaneously liberates humans to be humane.[92]

Common to theologians of this type is a realization that the practical and theoretical issues facing academies, churches, and societies can only be met in an ongoing critical collaboration mediating the cries of the victims to those interested in transforming the structures of world and church. Both the reflex character of the relationship between theory and praxis and its question of norms involve a concomitant change (conversion) of social structures and consciousness. Such conversions—as ongoing withdrawals from bias and sin—are intrinsic to both genuine religious traditions of faith and to the realization of reason in human histories and societies. In varying and, I believe, complementary manners, they indicate how Marx's trust in philosophy as the context for a sublation into critical praxis transformative of the world was misplaced. Instead they join in the many struggles of victims as disclosive of the transformative powers intrinsic to the ongoing realizations of both religion and reason. These theologians are committed to concrete, ongoing "realizations" of religion and of reason in personal and social living which will promote a solidarity with victims and forms of praxis far more extensive and critical than philosophy alone could ever evoke.

## Conclusion

This survey of the relationships between theory and praxis in contemporary Christian theologies indicates the diversity and dialectical differences of present theological positions. Where the first type tends to identify theology with categories derived from (usually rather watered down forms of) classical theory, the second type tends to identify the task of theology in various forms of modern, more or less secular, praxis—even to the point of negating theology. The third type insists upon the nonidentity of theology in regard to any forms of theory-praxis, although it is hard pressed to articulate how that nonidentity is relational. The fourth type attempts theoretic correlations between the identity concerns of the first two types and the nonidentity concerns of the third; while the fifth type emphasizes that such correlations can be genuinely critical only if grounded in ongoing processes of conversion. I have indicated how the complementarities of the types are integrated within dialectical contradictions which, I am convinced, can only be adequately met by transforming the ways in which theology is done. If this chapter establishes anything, I would hope that it at least intimates how the relationship of theory and praxis goes right to the core of the entire theological enterprise.

## NOTES

1. Among the best treatments of theory-praxis in English are: R. Bernstein, *Praxis and Action: Contemporary Philosophies of Human Activity* (Philadelphia: University of Pennsylvania Press, 1971); J. Habermas, *Theory and Practice* (Boston: Beacon Press, 1973); N. Lobkowicz, *Theory and Practice: History of a Concept from Aristotle to Marx* (South Bend: University of Notre Dame Press, 1967); for a short presentation, cf. N. Lobkowicz, "Theory and Practice," in *Marxism, Communism and Western Civilization* (New York: Herder and Herder, 1973), vol. 3, pp. 160–79, and W. Post, "Theory and Prac-

tice," in *Sacramentum Mundi* (New York: Herder and Herder, 1970), vol. 6, pp. 246–49; also the literature referred to in n. 3 of chap. 2 above.

2. On the use of models or types, cf. H. Richard Niebuhr, *Christ and Culture* (New York: Harper, 1951) and A. Dulles, *Models of the Church* (New York: Doubleday, 1974). Here I am using the approach of D. Tracy's *Blessed Rage for Order: The New Pluralism in Theology* (New York: Seabury, 1975), pp. 22–42, where types or models attempt to articulate some aspects of B. Lonergan's dialectical horizon analysis; cf. his *Method in Theology* (New York: Herder and Herder, 1972), pp. 235ff.

3. Niebuhr, op. cit., p. 40.

4. The reflex character of theory-praxis is that both are of concrete, human subjects; hence, even in theorizing there is, as T. Adorno puts it, within its inmost cell that which is unlike thought. Praxis as human activity objectifies itself toward interpersonal or intersubjective life-worlds; when that orientation is denied or truncated, the objectifications of the activity are alienated and alienating, while the activity itself approximates mechanical technique, cf. J. Habermas, op. cit., pp. 253–82; and his *Knowledge and Human Interests* (Boston: Beacon Press, 1971), pp. 301–17 on the relation of modern technocracy to "pure theory." Since both theory and praxis are of the subject, one can see why theory cannot sublate praxis although praxis can sublate theory inasmuch as "objectivity is self-transcending subjectivity"; cf. Lonergan, op. cit., pp. 265, 292.

5. On Aristotle, cf. Lobkowicz, *Theory and Practice*, pp. 3–33; on Hegel, cf. M. Riedel, *Theorie und Praxis im Denken Hegels* (Stuttgart: Kohlhammer, 1965), pp. 136–63; on both thinkers, cf. J. Ritter, *Metaphysik und Politik* (Frankfurt: Suhrkamp, 1969).

6. For an overview of this tendency, cf. G. Radnitzky, *Contemporary Schools of Metascience*, 2nd rev. ed. (Göteborg: Akademiförlaget, 1970). The Frankfurt School sees this tendency as present in the positions of Karl Popper's "critical rationalism" and in N. Luhmann's system-theory; cf. T. Adorno et al., *Der Positivismusstreit in der deutschen Soziologie* (Berlin: Luchterhand, 1969) and J. Habermas with N. Luhmann, *Theorie der Gesellschaft oder Sozialtechnologie* (Frankfurt: Suhrkamp, 1971). On the relations of this tendency to theology, cf. W. Pannenberg, *Theology and the Philosophy of Science*, trans. F. McDonagh (Philadelphia: Westminster Press, 1976), pp. 29–50.

7. In my opinion this tendency embraces those efforts aimed at disclosing the basis of all human activity in human intersubjective performance; it would include the trends discussed by R. Bernstein, op. cit., as well as the hermeneutical, dialectical, and transcendental trends; cf. Radnitzky, op. cit.; Karl-Otto Apel, *Transformation der*

*Philosophie,* 2 vols. (Frankfurt: Suhrkamp, 1973); *Continuum* 8/1–2 (Spring–Summer 1970): 3–133; I. Lakatos and A. Musgrave (eds.), *Criticism and the Growth of Knowledge* (Cambridge: University Press, 1970).

8. This is clear from Lobkowicz's history, cf. op. cit. For more contemporary discussion, cf. M. Horkheimer, *Die Sehnsucht nach dem ganz Anderen* (Hamburg: Furche, 1970); W. Oelmüller, "The Limitations of Social Theories," in J. Moltmann, J. B. Metz, et al., *Religion and Political Society* (New York: Harper & Row, 1974), pp. 127–69; and M. Theunissen, *Gesellschaft und Geschichte* (Berlin: W. de Gruyter & Co., 1969).

9. Sacralism or sacralization does not imply an interpersonal appropriation of religious meanings and values, but that religious symbol-systems were used, irrespective of differentiating religious experience, to legitimate imperial or feudal social orders, cf. E. Voegelin, *The Ecumenic Age* (Baton Rouge: Louisiana State University Press, 1974), pp. 36–58, 114–17.

10. Cf. E. Voegelin, op. cit., pp. 260–66; also his *From Enlightenment to Revolution* (Durham: Duke University Press, 1975); O. Marquard, *Schwierigkeiten mit der Geschichtsphilosophie* (Frankfurt: Suhrkamp, 1973), deals with the problems of secularist undifferentiation in philosophy; regarding the problems in theology, cf. M. Xhaufflaire and K. Derksen (eds.), *Les deux visages de la théologie de la sécularisation* (Tournai: Casterman, 1970).

11. Cf. E. Voegelin, *The Ecumenic Age,* pp. 300–35; B. Lonergan, op. cit., pp. 85–99, 302–20.

12. Cf. Lonergan, op. cit., pp. 128ff., 235–66; also M. Marković, *From Affluence to Praxis: Philosophy and Social Criticism* (Ann Arbor: University of Michigan Press, 1974), pp. 1–44; as this relates to a transcendental, praxis-grounded linguistic usage, cf. K.-O. Apel, op. cit., vol. 2, pp. 311–435.

13. Cf. Gregory Baum, "The Impact of Sociology on Catholic Theology," *Catholic Theological Society of America Proceedings* 13 (1975): 1–29; also C. Davis, *Body as Spirit: The Nature of Religious Feeling* (New York: Seabury, 1976), pp. 159ff.

14. Insofar as dialectical analysis overcomes the false dichotomies of an empiricist reduction of ideas to "nothing but" materially observable phenomena (whether natural or social) and of an idealist reification of ideas into a realm of their own, such a dialectical analysis is open to ongoing further determinations, cf. Lonergan, op. cit., pp. 129f.

15. A relation is internal when a change in the relation changes the base; it is external when a change in the relation does not change the base. Cf. Lonergan, *Insight: A Study of Human Understanding,* rev. ed. (New York: Philosophical Library, 1958), pp. 343, 493.

16. Critical correlation types acknowledge, in different manners, that a relation of nonidentity need not be an external or extrinsic relation, cf. Lonergan, *Insight,* pp. 728f.

17. Tracy, op. cit., p. 24.

18. Cf. K. Rahner, "Theology," in *Sacramentum Mundi* 6, pp. 233–46; B. Lonergan, *Method in Theology,* pp. xi, 124, 301f., 315, 326, 363.

19. Cf. Lonergan, *Collection* (New York: Herder and Herder, 1967), pp. 252–67; also his *A Second Collection* (Philadelphia: Westminster Press, 1974), pp. 55–67; D. Tracy, *The Achievement of Bernard Lonergan* (New York: Herder & Herder, 1970), p. 88.

20. N. Lobkowicz, *Theory and Practice,* pp. 5–9, 26–57, 70–8.

21. Ibid., p. 74.

22. *Authority in the Church: A Study in Changing Paradigms* (Missoula: Scholar's Press, 1974).

23. Ibid., pp. 108–28; also Metz in *Religion and Political Society,* pp. 197–99.

24. *Distinguish to Unite or the Degrees of Knowledge* (New York: Scribner's, 1959), p. 136.

25. Ibid.

26. Ibid., pp. 247ff.

27. Ibid., p. 459.

28. *Integral Humanism* (Notre Dame: University Press, 1973), pp. 90ff.

29. Ibid., pp. 151ff.

30. Tracy, *Blessed Rage,* p. 25.

31. Ibid., pp. 25–6.

32. Ibid, pp. 31f. Also, Xhaufflaire and Derksen, op. cit., pp. 157–72.

33. Cf. W. Pannenberg, op. cit., pp. 249–55.

34. Ibid., pp. 111–17.

35. *Cross Currents* 17 (1967): 283–315.

36. Cf. A Dulles, *Revelation Theology* (New York: Herder & Herder, 1972), p. 169, where Dulles is describing Fontinell's position; cf. also the articles by J. Connelly and A. Dulles, along with the responses in *Catholic Theological Society of America Proceedings* 29 (1974): 1–123.

37. Van A. Harvey, *The Historian and the Believer* (New York: Macmillan, 1966), esp. pp. 204–91.

38. Cf. D. L. Mueller, *An Introduction to the Theology of A. Ritschl* (Philadelphia: Westminster, 1969).

39. Cf. W. Rauschenbusch, *A Theology for the Social Gospel* (New York: Abingdon Press, 1945, renewed copr. ed.).

40. *The Secular City: Secularization and Urbanization in Theological Perspective* (New York: Macmillan, 1965), p. 83.

41. Ibid., p. 261.

42. Cf. Ben van Onna and Martin Stankowski (eds.), *Kritischer Katholizismus: Argumente gegen die Kirchen-Gesellschaft* (Frankfurt: Fischer, 1969). This movement no longer exists, but some of its members produced important works, e.g., M. Xhaufflaire, *Feuerbach et la théologie de sécularisation* (Paris: Cerf, 1970); and F. v. d. Oudenrijn, *Kritische Theologie als Kritik der Theologie: Theorie und Praxis bei Marx als Herausforderung der Theologie* (Munich: Kaiser, 1972). For a summary presentation of these positions, cf. Charles Davis, "Theology and Praxis," *Cross Currents* 23 (1973): 154–68. The positions espoused in Critical Catholicism were not self-critical enough to sustain a long-term involvement in transforming church and society. Many genuine concerns, however, are now taken up and transformed in the "Church from Below" movement which draws on theologies of the fifth type; cf. R. Siebert, "The Church of the Future—The Church from Below: Küng and Metz," *Cross Currents* 31 (1981): 62–84. I believe parallels could be drawn between the history of the Critical Catholicism movement and that now going on among more radical feminists who would use feminist categories radically to negate all previous forms of theology; cf. Mary Daly, *Gyn/Ecology: The Metaethics of Radical Feminism* (Boston: Beacon Press, 1978).

43. Cf. Xhaufflaire and Derksen (eds.), op. cit., pp. 75–79, 157ff. For the exchanges of T. Altizer and E. Voegelin, cf. *Journal of the American Academy of Religion* 43 (1975): 757–72.

44. V. d. Oudenrijn, op. cit., pp. 158–65, 177–79. Oudenrijn criticizes Marx's critique of religion insofar as Marx considered the critique completed when he exposed the "bad theory" or theology of Hegel's thought.

45. C. Davis, "Theology and Praxis," pp. 164 and 167.

46. The merit of these theologians, in my opinion, is that they warn us against a too facile neglect of the real import of Marxist critique. Taking Marx with radical seriousness, however, involves not only interpreting him but changing him; and in this task they have not, I believe, explored sufficiently the inner contradictions of Marx's mediation of theory and praxis; cf. the penetrating study of D. Böhler, *Metakritik der Marxschen Ideologiekritik: Prolegomenon zu einer reflektierten Ideologiekritik und Theorie-Praxis Vermittlung* (Frankfurt: Suhrkamp, 1971).

47. Tracy, *Blessed Rage*, pp. 27–31. In designating this type as the primacy of faith-love I not only intend to designate the respective emphases of Barth and von Balthasar but also to indicate how the nonidentity they insist upon vis-à-vis theory and praxis is capable of being integrated within the critical correlations of the next two types.

48. Cf. W. Pannenberg, op. cit., pp. 266–77.

49. Ibid., pp. 270ff.

50. Von Balthasar, *Love Alone* (New York: Herder and Herder, 1969), p. 43.

51. Cf. von Balthasar's *Word and Revelation* (New York: Herder and Herder, 1964), pp. 57–163, and his *Word and Redemption* (New York: Herder and Herder, 1965), pp. 7–22, 109–26.

52. Cf. *Herrlichkeit: Eine theologische Ästhetik* (Einsiedeln: Johannes Verlag, 1966–67), III, 1, pp. 276ff., 706ff.; III, 2, 1, pp. 11–28.

53. Cf. *Love Alone*, pp. 51–125; *Word and Redemption*, pp. 49–86.

54. Cf. von Balthasar, *Prometheus: Studien zur Geschichte des deutschen Idealismus* (Heidelberg: Kerle, 1947), pp. 695–734, esp. p. 716, where von Balthasar articulates Kierkegaard's notion of paradox as an inescapable nonidentity in Christianity. Compare this with *Herrlichkeit* III, 2, 1, pp. 12f. for the strong similarity. Insofar as God is "undialectical," Metz is right in saying that Barth's theology (and I would add von Balthasar's) is paradoxical rather than dialectical, cf. Metz, "Politische Theologie," in *Sacramentum Mundi* (Freiburg: Herder, 1969), 3, col. 1239.

55. Tracy's observation that political theologians seem to have transformed the neoorthodox model (*Blessed Rage*, p. 242) needs clarification. Insofar as they insist upon a nonidentity, the political theologians are no different than Tracy and the others I shall discuss in my fourth type. The key question is how they mediate that nonidentity in terms of theory and praxis, and since they do not do so through supernaturalist paradox they are not in the primacy of faith-love or neoorthodox type.

56. R. Bernstein, *Praxis and Action*, pp. 96–122: "We may have thought that 'to be a Christian' along with other existential possibilities that Kierkegaard has poetically presented, demands inward action on *our* part. But in the end, the faith demanded to be a Christian is not what it appears to be, it is not something of our own doing. Only those 'kept alive in a state of death' are 'ripe for Eternity', only they—and this is the most incomprehensible of all human paradoxes—are prepared to be saved by God's grace" (p. 122).

57. Cf. P. Hart (ed.), *Thomas Merton, Monk* (New York: Sheed and Ward, 1974); F. Kelly, *Man Before God: T. Merton on Social Responsibility* (New York: Doubleday, 1974).

58. P. Berger and R. Neuhaus (eds.), *Against the World for the World: The Hartford Appeal and the Future of American Religion* (New York: Seabury, 1976).

59. Tracy, *Blessed Rage*, pp. 29–34.

60. Cf. A. Malet, *Mythos et Logos: La pensée de R. Bultmann* (Geneva: Fides, 1962); G. Greshake, *Historie wird Geschichte* (Essen: Ludgerus Verlag, 1963), pp. 60–84; D. Sölle, *Politische Theologie: Auseinandersetzung mit R. Bultmann* (Stuttgart: Kreuz, 1971).

61. P. Tillich, *Systematic Theology* (Chicago: University of Chicago Press, 1967), vol. 1, p. 93. Also his *Political Expectation* (New York: Harper & Row, 1971), edited from his early writings by James L. Adams.

62. Cf. C. Kegley and R. Bretall (eds.), *The Theology of P. Tillich* (New York: Macmillan, 1964), pp. 27–31, 100–5, 336ff. Also Tillich, *Systematic Theology*, vol. 2, pp. 90–94, esp. p. 91: "The tools of theology are rational, dialectical, and paradoxical; they are not mysterious in speaking of the divine mystery. The theological paradox is not 'irrational.'"

63. Cf. K. Fischer, *Der Mensch als Geheimnis: Die Anthropologie K. Rahners* (Freiburg: Herder, 1974), pp. 389–99; K. Rahner, *Schriften zur Theologie* (Einsiedeln: Benziger, 1970), pp. 519–90, and his *The Shape of the Church to Come* (New York: Seabury, 1975).

64. Cf. F. Fiorenza, "Critical Social Theory and Christology," in *CTSA Proceedings* 30 (1975): 80; on Pannenberg's differences from Moltmann, cf. M. Meeks, *Origins of the Theology of Hope* (Philadelphia: Fortress Press, 1974), pp. 64ff.

65. Op. cit., pp. 312f. This is my translation from the German. Compare this with Pannenberg, *Offenbarung als Geschichte*, 3rd ed. (Göttingen: Vandenhoeck & Ruprecht, 1965), pp. 136–48.

66. *Wissenschaftstheorie und Theologie*, p. 317.

67. Ibid., pp. 303–48.

68. Ibid., pp. 426–42, esp. pp. 437ff.

69. Tracy, *Blessed Rage*, pp. 52–56.

70. Ibid., pp. 64–87.

71. Cf. Tracy, *The Analogical Imagination* (New York: Crossroad, 1981), pp. 69–82, 390–98. Cf. this with *Blessed Rage*, pp. 242–46.

72. These distinctions are only analogously similar to the distinctions of natural or philosophical theology (represented in the academy), mythical theology (represented in the poets and theatre drama), and civil theology (represented in political publics) made by Varro; the differences are, of course, very great; cf. *The Analogical Imagination*, pp. 3–98 and E. Feil, "Von der 'politischen Theologie' zur 'Theologie der Revolution'?" in E. Feil and R. Weth (eds.), *Diskussion zur "Theologie der Revolution"* (Munich: Kaiser, 1969), pp. 110–32; and F. Fiorenza, "Political Theology as Foundational Theology," in *Catholic Theological Society of America Proceedings* 32 (1977): 142–77, esp. pp. 148–54. Augustine discusses Varro's divisions in *City of God*, trans. H. Bettenson (New York: Penquin Books, 1972), pp. 234–90. From the perspective of critical praxis correlations, it could be argued that Tracy's distinctions between foundational, systematic, and practical theologies are not so much distinct disciplines as they are efforts to articulate, within what Lonergan would term "the foundational specialty" of theology, the general and special categories relative to intellectual, religious, and moral conversion processes. Note the parallels between Tracy's distinctions of the three disciplines and the three orientations of Pannenberg (academy), Rahner (church), and Metz (society), discussed and related to Loner-

gan's work in Michael O'Callaghan, *Unity in Theology: Lonergan's Framework for Theology in its New Context* (Washington, D.C.: University of America Press, 1980), pp. 1–64, 457–81.

73. Tracy is clearly concerned with the alienations and distortions evident in the academic, ecclesial, and social publics; cf. *The Analogical Imagination*, pp. 339–404. Those which he mentions, as well as those discussed above in chaps. 1 and 2, would seem to me to lead to an understanding of the transcendental orientations toward the true, the beautiful, and the good as primarily orientations of reason as *not yet* realized in those publics. The classics especially never claim to be the full realization of these transcendentals. To take the most theologically difficult example, the classic event of Jesus is constituted by his being, preaching, and praxis of manifesting, proclaiming, and living out an eschatological vocation to the Kingdom of God as always-already-not-yet realized in humankind; cf. ibid., pp. 305–38.

74. Cf. *The Analogical Imagination*, pp. 81f. Note well that I am *not* saying that Tracy does not take stands in this truly brilliant work—quite the contrary, he takes very well argued stands. What I am saying is that the conceptual framework of his threefold distinction between foundational, systematic, and practical disciplines does not seem to me to be adequate for the stands he does take. I believe that the *functional* differentiations of Lonergan would be more adequate to Tracy's actual performance as recorded in this work, rather than Tracy's own attempts to fit his stands into his revised definitions of the previous distinctions between fundamental, systematic, and practical theologies. For those distinctions, however finely revised, seem to me to be inadequate to the demands of doing theology in our time; cf. Lamb, *History, Method and Theology* (Missoula: Scholars Press, 1978), pp. 506 ff. Also Frederick Lawrence, "Method and Theology as Hermeneutical," in M. Lamb (ed.), *Creativity and Method: Essays in Honor of B. Lonergan* (Milwaukee: Marquette Univ. Press, 1981), pp. 79–104. It is in this sense that I believe the distinctions between the fourth and fifth types are important; cf. William Shea, "Matthew Lamb's Five Models of Theory-Praxis and the Interpretation of John Dewey's Pragmatism," *Catholic Theological Society of America Proceedings* 32 (1977): 125–41. As I discuss in chap. 5 below, I believe that Lonergan's method provides a framework for coming to terms with the issues of theory and praxis raised since Hegel and Marx.

75. Praxis, in this type, refers to all fields of human doing or performance (e.g., symbolic, psychic, cognitive, moral, economic, political, social, cultural, religious). Theology can be done at the level our times demand, therefore, only if it undertakes both a critical collaboration with other fields of human inquiry and a critical collaboration with those whose freedom is denied or alienated. For freedom is con-

stitutive of genuine praxis insofar as genuine praxis is the living out of
the transcendental imperatives of attentiveness, intelligence, reasonableness, responsibility, and love. That is, praxis has its own intrinsic
norms and hence is critically "counterfactual" when the facts are the
alienations and exploitation of human beings within dehumanizing,
unjust systems or structures; cf. Lamb, *History, Method and Theology*,
pp. 2–210; Lonergan, *Method in Theology*, pp. 20–25; J. Habermas,
*Theory and Practice*, pp. 253–82; also the references discussed in the
section on praxis and generalized empirical method in chap. 5 of this
book.

76. Cf. T. Adorno, *Negative Dialectics*, trans. E. B. Ashton (New
York: Seabury, 1973), pp. 334–38; W. Becker, *Hegels Begriff der Dialektik und das Prinzip des Idealismus* (Stuttgart: Kohlhammer, 1969),
pp. 44–85; H. Peukert, *Wissenschaftstheorie-Handlungstheorie-Fundamentale Theologie* (Frankfurt: Suhrkamp, 1978), pp. 213–31,
241–99; M. Theunissen, *Sein und Schein: Die kritische Funktion der
Hegelschen Logik* (Frankfurt: Suhrkamp, 1980), pp. 13–19, 301–486.

77. In terms of the understanding of praxis presented in theologians
of the fifth type, it would be a misunderstanding of praxis to attempt
to ground it in anything approaching "pure practical reason." Thus
Metz can speak of the "primacy of praxis" without thereby intending
the understandings of praxis operative in the second type discussed
above; cf. his *Faith in History and Society: Toward a Practical Fundamental Theology* (New York: Crossroad, 1980), pp. 49–83. By "pure
practical reason" I understand both the Kantian articulation of the
same *and*, more importantly, how theologies of the second type are
not sufficiently critical of the secular forms of praxis they adopt, as
though those forms were "pure" or innocent of victimizing human
beings. On the need to express our solidarity with the victims of the
past by not surrendering the traditions to those in power, cf. Elizabeth Fiorenza's response to Charles Davis, "Is the Church an Idol?"
*Commonweal* 1 February 1980, pp. 52f.; also her "Toward a Feminist
Biblical Hermeneutics," in D. Richesen and B. Mahan (eds.), *The
Challenge of Liberation Theology: A First World Response* (Maryknoll: Orbis, 1981).

78. Cf. Lonergan, *Method in Theology*, pp. 24, 125–45, 332, 355–68.

79. Cf. Johann B. Metz and Trutz Rendtorff (eds.), *Die Theologie in
der Interdisziplinären Forschung* (Düsseldorf: Bertelsmann, 1971). At
this writing it appears that the Bielefeld project will not be realized
now due to the procrastination of the ecclesial authorities in West
Germany in giving the necessary authorization.

80. On Habermas's resignation from the Max Planck Institute, cf.
Jürgen Habermas, "Warum ich die Max-Planck-Gesellschaft ver-
lasse," in *Die Zeit*, no. 20 (15 May 1981): 19.

81. Cf. Lonergan, *Method in Theology*, p. 137; also his "The Ongoing Genesis of Methods," *Studies in Religion* 6/4 (1977): 341, 351

82. Cf. Lonergan, *Insight,* pp. xvii, 115–28, 225–42, 387–90, 616–33, 718–29; *Method in Theology,* pp. 3–25.

83. Cf. chap. 5 of this book and the references given in it to Lonergan's works.

84. Cf. Robert Doran, "Theological Grounds for a World-Cultural Humanity," in M. Lamb (ed.), *Creativity and Method,* pp. 105–22; also Doran's *Psychic Conversion and Theological Foundations: Toward a Reorientation of the Human Sciences* (Missoula: Scholars Press, 1981); William Mathews, "Method and the Social Appropriation of Reality," in Lamb (ed.), *Creativity and Method,* pp. 425–42.

85. Cf. Thomas McCarthy, *The Critical Theory of Jürgen Habermas* (Cambridge, Mass: MIT Press, 1978), pp. 75–90, 193–213, 232–71, 351, and the references to Habermas's works given there. On the relation of Kolberg's work to Lonergan, cf. Walter Conn, "Moral Development: Is Conversion Necessary?" in M. Lamb (ed.), *Creativity and Method,* pp. 307–24; also Conn's *Conscience: Development and Self-Transcendence* (Birmingham: Religious Education Press, 1981).

86. Cf. Thomas McCarthy, op. cit., pp. 272–386; Karl-Otto Apel, *Towards a Transformation of Philosophy,* trans. Glyn Adey and David Frisby (Boston: Routledge and Kegan Paul, 1980), pp. 136–79, 225–300. On the self-correcting process of learning, cf. Lonergan, *Insight,* 174f., 286f., 289–91, 300, 303, 706, 713–18. On the relevance of this to the realization of philosophy, cf. Mark Morelli, "Horizonal Diplomacy," in M. Lamb (ed.), *Creativity and Method,* pp. 459–74.

87. Cf. chaps. 4 and 5 of this book; also Joseph Komonchak, "Lonergan and the Tasks of Ecclesiology," in Lamb (ed.), *Creativity and Method,* pp. 265–74; Michael Gibbons, "Insight and Emergence: An Introduction to Lonergan's Circulation Analysis," ibid., pp. 529–42; and Philip McShane, "Generalized Empirical Method and the Actual Context of Economics," ibid., pp. 543–72.

88. Cf. the early differences between political and liberation theologies as articulated by Francis Fiorenza, "Political Theology and Liberation Theology," in T. McFadden (ed.), *Liberation, Revolution and Freedom* (New York: Seabury, 1975), pp. 3–29. Compare with the more recent work of Metz, *The Emergent Church,* trans. Peter Mann (New York: Crossroad, 1981), and *Unterbrechungen* (Gütersloh: Gerd Mohn, 1981), pp. 74–84.

89. Cf. n. 79 above; also Helmut Peukert, *Wissenschaftstheorie-Handlungstheorie-Fundamentale Theologie,* pp. 300–56; M. Lamb, *History, Method and Theology,* pp. 357–536.

90. Cf. Metz, *The Emergent Church,* pp. 1–16, 48–106; also Jürgen Moltmann, *The Church in the Power of the Spirit: A Contribution to Messianic Ecclesiology,* trans. Margaret Kohl (New York: Harper & Row, 1977); also Moltmann's *The Trinity and the Kingdom: The Doc-*

*trine of God,* trans. Margaret Kohl (New York: Harper & Row, 1981).

91. Cf. Johann B. Metz, *Unterbrechungen,* pp. 29–42; Gregory Baum, *Catholics and Canadian Socialism* (New York: Paulist, 1980); Judith Plaskow, "Christian Feminism and Anti-Judaism," *Cross Currents* 28 (1978):306–9; Elizabeth Fiorenza, "Early Christian History in a Feminist Perspective," *Cross Currents* 29 (1979): 301–23; Carol P. Christ, *Diving Deep and Surfacing: Women Writers on Spiritual Quest* (Boston: Beacon Press, 1980); Rosemary Ruether, *Liberation Theology: Human Hope Confronts Christian History and American Power* (New York: Paulist Press, 1972); and the contributions in Rosemary Ruether and Eleanor McLaughlin (eds.), *Women of Spirit: Female Leadership in the Jewish and Christian Traditions* (New York: Simon and Schuster, 1979). On the hermeneutical presuppositions of these critical recoveries of scripture, cf. Sandra M. Schneiders, "From Exegesis to Hermeneutics: The Problem of the Contemporary Meaning of Scripture," *Horizons* 8 (1981): 23–39.

92. Cf. the references to liberation theologians given in chaps. 1 and 2 of this book. Since most of the Latin American liberation theological books which deal with critical methodological issues have not yet been translated from Spanish or Portuguese, there seems to be a tendency among North American critics to presume that they do not critically reflect upon the positions they take; cf. Schubert Ogden, *Faith and Freedom: Toward a Theology of Liberation* (Nashville: Abingdon, 1979), pp. 30–39. I doubt that Ogden's criticisms will go unchallenged by anyone who reads the following: Jon Sobrino et al., *Método teológico y cristología latinoamericana* (San Salvador, 1975); Enrique Dussel, *Método para una filosofia de la liberación* (Salamanca: Sígueme, 1974); Raúl Vidales, *Cuestiones en torno al método en la teología de la liberación* (Lima: Secretariado Latino-americana, 1974); Juan Carlos Scannone, *Teología de la liberación y praxis popular: Aportes críticos para una teología de la liberación* (Salamanca: Sígueme, 1976); Clodovis Boff, *Teologia e Prática: Teologia do Político e suas Mediações* (Petrópolis: Vozes, 1978). There are also three important articles by Latin American liberation theologians in Karl Rahner (ed.), *Befreiende Theologie* (Stuttgart: Kohlhammer, 1977): Leonardo Boff, "Theologie der Befreiung—die hermeneutischen Voraussetzungen" (pp. 46–61); Juan Carlos Scannone, "Das Theorie-Praxis Verhältnis in der Theologie der Befreiung" (pp. 77–96); and Jon Sobrino, "Theologisches Erkennen in der europäischen und der lateinamerikanischen Theologie" (pp. 123–43). There was also a major meeting on theological method in Latin American theology held in Mexico City in 1975 which issued a year later in a 658 page volume: *Liberación y Cautiverio: Debates en torno al método de la teología en America Latina* (Mexico City: Comité Organizador, 1976). Francisco Quijano's article in this book, "El Método Transcendental en Teo-

logía," pp. 375–408, outlines some of the contributions Lonergan's method would make to Latin American liberation theology. The general debates regarding Quijano's proposals (ibid., pp. 515–20, 523, 526, 532–35, 548f.) indicate how some of the participants misunderstood Lonergan's method as an exercise in logical formalism. On the misrepresentations of liberation theology in Dennis McCann's *Christian Realism and Liberation Theology* (Maryknoll: Orbis, 1981), cf. Matthew Lamb, "A Distorted Interpretation of Latin American Liberation Theology," *Horizons* 8 (Fall 1981). Of course, the Latin Americans have no monopoly on liberation theology; there are Asian, African, Feminist, American Native, American Hispanic, Black, and Ecological liberation theologies. Common to all of them is an uncommon attentiveness to the victims of widespread contemporary injustice.

# Chapter 4

# Political Theology and Enlightenment

*Toward a Reconstruction of Dogma as Socially Critical*

**P**olitical and liberation theologies are initiating a new framework for understanding the task of theology. The previous chapter indicated how the relationship of theory and praxis is foundationally significant for the ways in which theology is done. If praxis is not merely the application of theological theories in pastoral or ethical practice but is also the foundation of all theological understanding, then theologies committed to praxis have the noetic task of showing how a praxis-grounded theology would reconstruct the past history of theology. Church doctrine, or dogma, seems to pose a stumbling block in such reconstruction. Modernity appears to have replaced the authority of dogma with the authority of experience. In this chapter I should like to indicate some of the categories capable of meeting the issues of reconstructing the dogmatic past of theology. In the next chapter these will be more fully developed in relation to Lonergan's work on method in theology.

The emergence of church doctrines is associated with the impact upon Christianity of the logos or conceptuality of Graeco-Roman cultures. Since the Enlightenment, with its critiques of both that conceptuality and Christianity in the name of a new empirical rationality, theologians have faced a dilemma: either dogma or experience. To accept one as normative meant minimizing or rejecting the other as normative. Some theologians opted for the more experiential forms of modern knowledge (for example, naturalism, Ritschlianism, liberalism, modernism);

others sought to preserve dogmatic faith either by bypassing the Enlightenment (for example, fundamentalism, fideism) or by insisting upon the validity of classical conceptuality against the claims of modernity (for example, Protestant neoorthodoxy, Catholic neoscholasticism). This chapter will first briefly sketch a few main criticisms of efforts to solve this dilemma, and then outline a possible response to it in terms of political theology and three different forms of enlightenment.

### Dogma Versus Experience?

In spite of many creative theological efforts aimed at adapting traditional dogmas to modern experience (for example, Schleiermacher, Blondel, Chardin, Bultmann, Rahner, Tillich, and the Niebuhrs), serious doubts are still raised about the validity of such mediations. Four criticisms of these efforts are especially relevant to my subject.

Peter Berger's sociology of knowledge, with its appeals to an empirically given "everyday consciousness" and the minority status of believers in secular society, leads him to insist on the alternatives confronting any theology today. Either one preserves one's religious traditions and confronts modern society critically, or one tries to assimilate those traditions into modernity and thereby risks jeopardizing them. As cognitive minorities in largely secular cultures, Berger sees no way out of this dilemma for contemporary theologies—although, as Berger expresses it, it is probably due as much to his undifferentiated two-kingdom Lutheran theology as to his sociology of knowledge.[1]

Eric Voegelin's philosophical critique of doctrinization is more cogent than Berger's critique of mediation. Voegelin does not oppose dogma to modern experience. Indeed, he sees much of modernity as the social and cultural offspring of "the general deformation of experiential symbols into doctrines."[2] The Trinitarian and Christological doctrines of the fourth and fifth centuries were derivative rather than experiential symbols, and conditioned by the theological debates of those times. This doctrinization was deformed into conceptual systems cut off from the true experience of theophanic reality expressed in the narrative or experiential symbols of the New Testament. Such conceptual doctrines, coupled with the hubris of political power, became "dogmatomachies" in Voegelin's terms: "This predominance of the doctrinal form has caused the modern phenomenon of the great dogmatomachies, that is, of the theological dogmatomachy, and the so-called wars of religion, in the sixteenth and seventeenth centuries A.D., and of the ideological dogmatomachy, and the corresponding revolutionary wars, from the eighteenth to the twentieth centuries A.D."[3]

Whereas late medieval scholasticism, nominalism, and Cartesianism set the stage for the theological dogmatomachy, it was above all Hegelianism that epitomized an age in revolt against theological and metaphysical dogmatism. Yet Hegel and the post-Hegelians did not recover an experience of reality as theophanic. Instead, they inverted doctrinal language and derailed experience into egophanic ideologies. Greek and biblical narratives, symbolizing the experience of reality as constituted in the tension between divinity and humanity (the *metaxy*), were degraded into mere projections of an immature self-awareness that is now superseded by "the egophanic God-man or superman (Feuerbach, Marx, Nietzsche)" who establishes "the final realm of freedom in history." These doctrinally derivative God-men or "Christs" can then "try to force the Parousia into history in their own person."[4]

Following a Heideggerian critique of Western metaphysics, Bernhard Welte suspects that Nicea, with its emphasis upon *ousia*, represents a conceptually static forgetfulness of being. Such a metaphysics has found its apotheosis in the technocracy of modernity's neopositivism and empiricism. If we are to recover the primordial experience of being, then we must criticize the history of Western metaphysics and recognize the limitations of the classical dogmas.[5]

In a similar vein, David Tracy argues for a revisionist approach to traditional doctrines in the light of criteria adequate to our human situation and contemporary experience. He finds classical Christian theism and any exclusivist Christology both inadequate and incoherent by such criteria.[6] Specifically, he criticizes the political theologies of praxis—such as those of

Moltmann, Metz, Alves, Shaull, Segundo, Gutiérrez, or Soelle—
for seeming to ignore this problematic. In Tracy's opinion, these
theologians use a transformed neoorthodox model which tends
to leave the traditional dogmas in their classical forms—as
though their insistence upon orthopraxis covers up their failure
to analyze orthodoxy critically.[7]

Whatever the diversity of perspectives among Berger, Voegelin, Welte, and Tracy, their various critiques of traditional
dogma, when viewed in the light of their respective positions,
agree in three respects: (1) that any adequate understanding of
human experience involves an intrinsic orientation to the transcendent as sacral; (2) that such an orientation is more com-
pactly expressed in biblical and other narratives, and may well
be lost in doctrinal conceptuality; and (3) that any reflection on
this problematic must, at least negatively, take seriously the impact of the Enlightenment on modernity.[8]

### The Transformative Dimension of Political Theology

I call "political" all those theologies which acknowledge that
human action, or praxis, is not only the goal but the foundation
of theory. The last chapter indicated how such praxis-grounded
and praxis-oriented theologies would include not only the political theology initiated by Metz but the theological method articulated by Lonergan, and various forms of liberation theology.[9]
These theologies are not simply neoorthodox, if by that one un-
derstands a model of theologizing similar to that of Karl Barth or
Hans Urs von Balthasar. For such neoorthodox theologies mediate Christian faith by means of supernaturalist paradoxes; the
emphasis is on how revelation so transcends reason that it in
some way negates rational experience. Political theology, on the
other hand, mediates faith dialectically, emphasizing how it
transforms human action.[10] Moreover, where political theologians emphasize the transformative character of religious truth,
Berger, Voegelin, Welte, and Tracy tend to emphasize its disclosive character. All four authors criticize the dogmatic as-
sumptions of neoorthodoxy. What they have not appreciated is
the insight of political theology into how neoorthodoxy represents the inadequacy of a disclosure model of truth to handle

dogma. Although these same authors criticize the tendency of neoorthodox theologies to minimize the value of empirical and/or historical-critical methods, on the one hand, and phenomenological or ontological reflection, on the other, they formulate their criticisms in terms of the disclosive possibilities of such methods or reflections vis-à-vis religious symbols. Where neoorthodoxy insists upon the disclosure criteria of revelation, our four authors insist upon the necessity of complementing or correlating revelatory symbols with empirical, historical-critical, phenomenological, or ontological disclosive criteria.

The disclosive methods of empirical research, phenomenological hermeneutics, historical-critical analysis, or ontological reflection certainly have contributions to make in theology. They are indispensable or helpful in disclosing the continuous contexts within which theology relates religious traditions to manifold personal, social, and cultural situations of the past and present. Political theology acknowledges this in its concern for interdisciplinary research (Metz), for the methods of the natural and human sciences (Peukert), for the value of the hermeneutical circle (Segundo) and sociological analysis (Baum) to theology, for the disclosive potential of Christian symbols in our contemporary situations (Gutiérrez, Metz, Moltmann, Hodgson). In terms of Lonergan's functional specialization, these disclosive methods are especially appropriate to the first phase of theology concerned with an ever more adequate mediation of the past with the present.[11]

But these disclosive methods cannot do full justice either to human experience or to church doctrines. The most such methods can disclose are the dialectically divergent horizons of meaning and value that issue in different results of research, different interpretations, contradictory historical analyses, opposed ontologies, variant societies. It is at this point that neoorthodoxy raises the banner of religious conversion as the sole criterion capable of disclosing ultimate truth. Humans cannot live from continually revised hypotheses alone. Church dogmatics (Barth) must disclose the true way by confronting human experience with its paradoxical need for religious faith, hope, and love. In criticizing this dogmatic stance, Berger, Tracy, Voegelin, and

Welte do not regress to liberal skepticism. Instead, they seek to articulate (much as Bultmann did vis-à-vis Barth) realms of human experience disclosive of transcendence. Through various appeals to limit-experiences (Berger, Tracy) and transcending-experiences (Voegelin, Welte), they seek the ontological foundations from which the doctrinal symbols of the past can be revised (Tracy) or radically relativized (Voegelin).

In the various perspectives of political theology these positions are inadequate in their criticisms of neoorthodoxy and in their appeals to human experience. A foundational approach to human experience is incomplete or inadequate if it attempts a merely disclosive ontology of limit-experience or transcending-experiences. For such an approach, no matter how sophisticated, minimizes the transformative effect of religious and doctrinal symbols on human experience. Unlike neoorthodoxy, political theology attends not only to the transformative import of religious and doctrinal symbols on human experience but also to the transformative structures or dynamics of human experience itself. When limit or transcendence are analyzed phenomenologically or ontologically, their negative and heuristic orientation to the future tends to be overlooked. Limit and transcendence are "disclosed" as dimensions or structures *already present* implicitly or explicitly in human experience.[12] When they are related to the future or to freedom, the latter are *not* presented as foundational to limit or transcendence but as their consequence or goal.[13] Political theology, however, approaches limit and transcendence as grounded in human praxis, as the latter is negatively constituted by limit and heuristically constituted by transcendence. Limit and transcendence are not disclosed as already present but are experienced as imperative challenges capable of transforming or converting the present unfreedom of human experience. There are many illustrations of this transformative dimension of foundations in political theology. Metz refers to praxis-oriented political theology as foundational theology, and to the way in which ontology masks the future. He and Moltmann elaborate the foundational importance of eschatology (future) and suffering (limit) for theology. Peukert carefully shows how both scientific theory and theology need foundations in a theory of communicative interaction as praxis. Latin American liberation theologians emphasize the actual contexts in which theology is produced. Lonergan sees the foundations of the second phase of functional specialization, concerned with the mediation of the present with the future, as articulating the imperatives of intellectual, moral, and religious conversions. Indeed, Lonergan's intentionality analysis is not so much phenomenologically disclosive as it is praxis-transformative, with its emphasis upon self-appropriation and the levels of conscious activity as imperatives toward transcendence.[14]

The experience of truth in this framework is primarily a transforming correspondence between subject and object, and only if transformation occurs (in either subject or object or both) is there a disclosure of truth. The transformation is praxis, where praxis is understood as conscious performance or doing in contrast both to production or making and to theory or definition. This distinguishes political theology's notion of praxis from materialistic or idealistic uses of the term. While Aristotle's distinction between *praxis* as human conduct or doing and *poiesis* as human production or making is relevant here, political theology reverses the primacy of theory over praxis. Where Aristotle subordinated *praxis* and *poiesis* to disclosive theory, political theology subordinates theory and production to praxis. Where Hegel sublates praxis and production into theory as absolute knowledge, political theology sublates theory and production into praxis as conscious and free performance.[15] Similarly, where Marx tends to sublate theory and praxis into production as materialist infrastructure, political theology sees this as a crypto-positivism in Marx's notion of praxis and insists that production should be sublated by praxis.[16]

This notion of human experience and action as primarily transformative has profound and widespread implications. Theory and definition, as well as production and making, are understood as disclosive consequences of a transformative or self-correcting process of learning.[17] Transformation is foundationally intrinsic to education and enlightenment whereas disclosure is derivative. This marks a radically new understanding of enlightenment inasmuch as attention is directed to the dialectically transformative praxis of enlightenment. This is radically new, not because transformative praxis was not operative in, for instance, the enlightenments associated with the Greek philosophical and medieval theological shifts toward theory, or in the modern Enlightenment with its shift toward empirically technical rationality. It is radically new since those enlightenments tended to control transformative praxis either by theory (classical) or by empirical technique (modern). Political theology is part of a contemporary enlightenment seeking to establish transformative praxis as the control of both theory and empirical technique.[18] For the sake of brevity, I shall sketch the different understandings of church doctrines or dogmas according to enlightenments successively giving priority first to theory, then to empirical technique, and finally to praxis.

### Three Enlightenments and Dogma

1. *A classical theoretical enlightenment* occurred in the medieval reception of Graeco-Roman theory in theology. In the twelfth and thirteenth centuries theology flourished as it incorporated more and more Hellenic and patristic notions into its commentaries, *quaestiones* and *summae*. If the Aristotelian notion of *episteme* influenced the schoolmen's ideal of scientific theory, their understanding of wisdom was drawn from patristic receptions of Middle Platonic and Neoplatonic notions of a hierarchy of being attained preeminently through contemplative *theoria*. These provided disclosive paradigms theoretically projecting and reflecting a hierarchical order in the spiritual and material universe, society, and the church. Theology as a speculative and practical science, subordinate to the vision of God as first Truth, hierarchically ordered the multiplicity of nature, human conduct, and revealed truths within the framework of a creative *exitus* and redemptive *reditus* to that Truth.[19] Church doctrines were understood as credal formulae or symbols disclosive of the church's faith in the revelation of the apostolic doctrines contained in sacred scripture. Biblical narrative and dogma were united in the schema of hierarchically revealed truths of faith. Hence, for Aquinas, the central Trinitarian and Christological mysteries were explicitly believed in by the major

figures in pre-Judaic and Old Testament times, although they had to veil those mysteries in figurative language for the less wise (*minores*) people of those times. The superior wisdom of the major figures was due to their hierarchical preeminence in the redemptive return of all things to God.[20] The doctrinal symbols, however, were not severed from the transformative experience of conversion, insofar as Aquinas, and even more Bonaventure, stressed the negative (*via negationis, pati divina*) and heuristic (for example, psychological analogy of the Trinity) aspects of participation in the ontological hierarchy.[21]

These negative and heuristic elements were increasingly sundered from experience in the perceptualism and logical pedantry of fourteenth-century scholasticism. If, as Peter Gay contends, "hierarchy" was the master metaphor of the Middle Ages, decadent scholasticism deformed the metaphysics of the metaphor into logical contradictions (for instance, Ockham's theological fideism legitimated the "papal tyranny" he politically abhorred). Mysticism retreated from the academic disputes of the schools, and, in the fifteenth century, Nicholas of Cusa could attempt to reinstate the hierarchical theophany of the universe only by privatizing it.[22] The subsequent Tridentine scholasticism of Cajetan, Cano, or Suarez solidified a conceptualistic doctrinization (in Voegelin's sense) that severed dogma from experiential symbols. The stage was set for an authoritarian practice of the hierarchical magisterium scarcely attentive to the transformative praxis of the *sensus fidelium*. Catholic manual theology was, in the limit, to become more subaltern to papal pronouncements than to God as first Truth.[23]

2. *A modern technical enlightenment,* from its tentative beginnings in the seventeenth and eighteenth centuries to its maturity in the nineteenth and twentieth centuries, removed the study of history from its tutelage to any metaphor of hierarchy (still so evident in Counter-Reformation writings) and gradually established the empirical criteria of historical-critical methods. Just as the empirical methods of the natural sciences replaced the primacy of classical theory, so the development of new empirical techniques replaced an interest in any divine hierarchical ordering of history (the *exitus-reditus* theme) with an interest in

history as *made* or *produced* by human action. Ranke's famous "how it actually happened" was not guided by a disclosive metaphor of hierarchical theory, but by a disclosive metaphor of empirical objectivity attentive to the human making of history. It was, if you will, a shift from the perspective of an Aristotelian theory disclosed by wisdom (*theoria, sophia*) to an Aristotelian notion of production or making disclosed by technique (*poiesis, techne*). Theory and praxis increasingly came under the aegis of empirical technique.[24]

Ever more refined methods of empirical research, contextual interpretation, and historical criticism immensely increased our knowledge of the historical background and composition of biblical narratives and church doctrines. But these methods tended to be techniques that studied such narratives or dogmas as *products,* as complexes of information, the origins and meanings of which could be disclosed irrespective of any religious stance of the researcher, interpreter, or historian. The gap between empirical rationality and religious assent widened as a succession of psychological (Freud), sociological (Comte, Marx), and historical-critical (Baur, Harnack, Wrede) approaches dissected scripture and church doctrines as merely human, culturally conditioned products, abstracted from any living relationship with converted religious conduct or transformative praxis. To be sure, there wasn't much of the latter visible in theological or hierarchical circles as spirituality continued its retreat into a private pietism. Secularism spread and, coupled with an industrial revolution that had subsumed empirical science into technology, challenged a whole series of religious traditions besides Christianity.[25]

A beleaguered Catholicism condemned all this as modernism, even though its own trusted theologians were treating church doctrines as products (albeit divinely revealed products—*depositum fidei*), applying to them the logical techniques of formal and virtual predication, explicit or implicit deduction.[26] So-called orthodoxy developed its own brand of the reliance on technique characteristic of liberalism or modernism. As the First World War disclosed how a technically enlightened humankind could put the products of its new knowledge at the service of its

old unconverted and unrepentant conduct (praxis), neoorthodoxy responded with its call to *metanoia*. Soon a series of mediational theologies (Bultmann, Teilhard de Chardin, Rahner, Tillich) made use of various historical ontologies to disclose creative relationships between the advances of empirical sciences
or scholarly techniques and traditional religious doctrines.[27]

3. A *contemporary praxis enlightenment* has its origins in some
nineteenth-century attempts to elaborate methods for the
human sciences distinct from those of the natural sciences. The
value-free pretensions of the modern technical enlightenment
are criticized. Merely disclosive models of truth are incomplete,
for what is disclosed may well be the alienating falsehood of biased theories, techniques, and human conduct (praxis) sedi-
mented in repressive social structures. If praxis as specifically
conscious human conduct is capable of deformed action when
controlled exclusively by theories or techniques, that praxis still
has imperative orientations to freedom which can be disclosed
only through transformative actions in accord with its imperatives. The ultimate arbiter amid conflicting theories and techniques can only be found in such transformative praxis. The
search for truth, then, has an intrinsic orientation to freedom
and responsibility as it struggles in the present to discern meaning and value.[28] Far from belittling the disclosive achievements
of the classical enlightenment, or the empirical methods of the
modern enlightenment, this praxis enlightenment attempts to
ground those achievements and methods in related and recurrent operations of social, intellectual, moral, and religious performance. It seeks to disclose their positive and negative aspects
by adverting to norms inherent in transformative praxis.[29]

Church doctrines or dogmas are not seen as only hierarchically revealed truths, nor simply as sociopsychological or cultural products, but as memories subversive of unfreedom (Metz),
as boundaries of ongoing educational traditions (Segundo), as
sets of meanings and values informing individual and collective
Christian living (Lonergan).[30] Theology becomes a critical co-
worker with other sciences, scholarly disciplines, pastoral and
social ministries. Together they seek to disclose and transform
the concrete personal, communal, social, political, and cultural

life forms within which Christians live out, or fail to live out, the transformative memories and values of their traditions. The objectivity of the truth of dogmas is conditioned by the transformative response of Christian praxis.[31]

Political theology, therefore, would see the criticisms of dogma by Berger, Tracy, Voegelin, and Welte as somewhat misplaced. The disclosive categories of phenomenology, ontology, or sociology of knowledge tend to overlook the orthopractical foundations of dogmas: the imperatives to change which they express. It is not sufficient to oppose doctrinal symbols to the experiential symbols of biblical narratives. For the latter, no less than the former, are in danger of congealing into static forms if their imperatives for transformation are not lived out in practice. Orthodoxy as "speaking the truth" is grounded in, and oriented toward, orthopraxy as "doing the truth."

Attention to the transformative dimensions of dogma can be found in Lonergan's *The Way to Nicea: The Dialectical Development of Trinitarian Theology* and in his essay on "The Origins of Christian Realism."[32] There are also Peterson's studies on how the Trinitarian and Christological doctrines expressed and called for a spirituality at odds with the centralizing ambitions of Roman imperial authority.[33] The relevance of these dogmas for our contemporary experience, the imperatives with which they challenge us, are expressed in the German Synod's *Confession of Faith in Hope* written by J. B. Metz. They are explored in J. Segundo's *Our Idea of God* and in F. Fiorenza's essay on "Critical Social Theory and Christology" and in other recent studies of the transformative dimensions of Christian living.[34] Much more work needs to be done. We have to know if, and how, church doctrines of the past brought Christian living critically to bear on the economic, social, and political conditions of their times. Unlike the historical analyses made under the aegis of modern enlightenment techniques, such studies, while using those techniques of historical scholarship, would not simply reduce doctrines to the plausibility structures of their historical context. Such reductionism would not do justice to the life forms of those who lived the doctrines. Instead, those studies would indicate if, and how, the dogmas expressed and promoted a praxis critical of the plausibility structures insofar as these hindered intellectual, moral, social, and/or religious development. Dogmas are expressive of a knowledge born of transformative religious love—a "love that is not to be just words or mere talk, but something real and active," a love "only by which we can be certain that we belong to the realm of the truth" (1 John 3:18f.). Insofar as dogmas are such a knowledge and we fail to live by them, our experience will be anathema.

## NOTES

1. P. Berger, "Zur Soziologie kognitiver Minderheiten," in *Internationale Dialog Zeitschrift* 2 (1969): 127–32; idem, *A Rumor of Angels* (New York: Doubleday, 1969); J. B. Metz (ed.), "Perspectives of a Political Ecclesiology," in *Concilium* 66 (1971): 7–23, 35–49, 50–81. Berger's undifferentiated two-kingdom theology is evident in his "Secular Theology and the Rejection of the Supernatural," in *Theological Studies* 38 (1977): 39–56, and "Responses to Peter Berger," by D. Tracy, S. Ogden, and L. Gilkey in *Theological Studies* 39 (1978): 486ff.

2. E. Voegelin, *The Ecumenic Age (Order and History IV)* (Baton Rouge: Louisiana State Univ. Press, 1974), pp. 48, 259–71.

3. Ibid., p. 48.

4. Ibid., pp. 261–62.

5. B. Welte, "Die Lehrformel von Nikaia und die abendländische Metaphysik," in B. Welte (ed.), *Zur Frühgeschichte der Christologie* (Freiburg: Herder, 1970), pp. 100–107.

6. D. Tracy, *Blessed Rage for Order* (New York: Seabury Press, 1975), pp. 64–87, 172–236.

7. Ibid., pp. 242–46. Tracy has corrected this misinterpretation of political and liberation theologians in his *The Analogical Imagination* (New York: Crossroad, 1981), pp. 69–82, 390–98. As I pointed out in the last chapter, neither theology can be properly understood as an extension of neoorthodoxy.

8. Cf. P. Berger, *The Sacred Canopy* (New York: Doubleday, 1967); idem, *A Rumor of Angels*, pp. 76ff.; Voegelin, op. cit., pp. 2–58; Welte, *Auf der Spur des Ewigen* (Freiburg: Herder, 1965), pp. 211–76, 380–426; Tracy, *Blessed Rage*, pp. 111–71.

9. Cf. the previous chap.; also Lamb, *History, Method and Theology* (Missoula: Scholars Press, 1978), pp. 2–114.

10. Ibid., pp. 19–52, 479–536.

11. B. Lonergan, *Method in Theology* (New York: Herder and Herder, 1972), pp. 125–45.

12. Berger, *Rumor*, pp. 52–75; Tracy, *Blessed Rage*, pp. 92–94; Voegelin, op. cit., pp. 6–11; Welte, *Im Spielfeld von Endlichkeit und Unendlichkeit* (Frankfurt: Herder, 1967).

13. Berger, *Rumor*, pp. 61–64; Tracy, *Blessed Rage*, pp. 210–11, 237–40, 244; Voegelin, op. cit., pp. 2–6, 333–35; Welte, *Dialektik der Liebe* (Frankfurt: Knecht, 1973), pp. 49–63.

14. Cf. Metz, "Political Theology," in *Sacramentum Mundi* (New York: Herder and Herder, 1970), 3, cols. 1232–40; idem, *Theology of the World* (New York: Herder and Herder, 1969), pp. 89ff., 99–116; Lamb, "Les implications methodologiques de la theologie politique," in M. Xhaufflaire (ed.), *La pratique de la theologie politique* (Tournai: Casterman, 1974), pp. 51–70; J. Moltmann, *The Crucified God* (New York: Harper & Row, 1974); Metz, "Erlösung und Emanzipation," in L. Scheffczyk (ed.), *Erlösung und Emanzipation* (Freiburg: Herder, 1973), pp. 120–40; H. Peukert, *Wissenschaftstheorie-Handlungstheorie-Fundamentale Theologie* (Frankfurt: Suhrkamp, 1978); J. Segundo, *The Liberation of Theology* (Maryknoll: Orbis, 1976); Lonergan, op. cit., pp. 3–55; idem, "Theology and Praxis," in *Catholic Theological Society of America Proceedings* 32 (1977): 1–20.

15. Cf. J. Ritter, *Metaphysik und Politik* (Frankfurt: Suhrkamp, 1969); R. Bernstein, *Praxis and Action* (Philadelphia: Univ. of Pennsylvania Press, 1971), pp. 11–83; J. Habermas, *Theory and Praxis* (Boston: 1973); K.-O. Apel, *Transformation der Philosophie* (Frankfurt: Suhrkamp, 1973), vol. 2, pp. 9–27, 9–154; Lamb, *History, Method and Theology*, pp. 56–114.

16. Cf. A Wellmer, *Critical Theory of Society* (New York: Herder and Herder, 1971); D. Böhler, *Metakritik der Marxschen Ideologiekritik* (Frankfurt: Suhrkamp, 1971); J. O'Neill (ed.), *On Critical Theory* (New York: Seabury, 1976).

17. Cf. Lonergan, *Insight: A Study of Human Understanding* (New York: Philosophical Library, 1957), pp. 174–75, 286–87, 289–91, 713–18; G. Baum, *Man Becoming* (New York: Herder and Herder, 1971).

18. Cf. C. Lenhardt, "The Wanderings of Enlightenment," in J. O'Neill (ed.), op. cit., pp. 34–57; Metz, Moltmann, Oemüller, *Religion and Political Society* (New York: Harper and Row, 1974); Habermas, op. cit., pp. 253–305.

19. Cf. M.-D. Chenu, *La théologie comme science au XIIIe siècle* (Paris: Cerf, 1943); L.-B. Geiger, *La participation dans la philosophie de S. Thomas d'Aquin* (Paris: Cerf, 1953); H. Parkes, *The Divine Order* (New York: Knopf, 1969); J. Wright, *The Order of the Universe in the Theology of St. Thomas Aquinas* (Rome: Gregorian Univ. Press, 1957).

20. T. Aquinas, *Summa Theologiae* II-II, 2, 6-8; this hierarchical

ordering also affected Aquinas's understanding of prudence; ibid., II-II, 47, 12.

21. Cf. J. Hochstaffl, *Negative Theologie* (Darmstadt: Wissenschaftliche Buchgesellschaft, 1976); B. Lonergan, *Verbum: Word and Idea in Aquinas* (Notre Dame Univ. Press, 1967); J. B. Metz, *Christliche Anthropozentrik* (Munich: Kösel, 1962).

22. Cf. P. Gay, *The Enlightenment* (New York: Knopf, 1966), pp. 242ff.; F. Copleston, *Late Medieval and Renaissance Philosophy* (New York: Doubleday-Anchor, 1963), vol. 1, pp. 74–107, 132f., 193–218; vol. 2, 37–54; K. Michalski, *La philosophie au XIV$^e$ siècle*, ed. K. Flasch (Frankfurt: 1969).

23. Cf. T. Sanks, *Authority in the Church: A Study in Changing Paradigms* (Missoula: Scholars Press, 1974); M. Seckler, "Die Theologie als kirchliche Wissenschaft nach Pius XII und Paul VI," in *Tübinger Theol. Quartalschrift*, 149 (1969): 209–34.

24. Cf. H. Barnes, *A History of Historical Writing* (New York: Dover, 1962), pp. 136–276; on Ranke's notion of power as disclosive of freedom, cf. H.-G. Gadamer, *Truth and Method* (New York: Seabury, 1975), pp. 178–87; on the empiricist fallacy underlying the notion of "making" history, cf. Lamb, *History, Method and Theology*, pp. 73–92, 120–36, 249–54, 341–56; on the pervasiveness of technique, cf. J. Ellul, *The Technological Society* (New York: Vintage Books, 1964).

25. Cf. Habermas, "Dogmatism, Reason and Decision: On Theory and Praxis in our Scientific Civilization," in op. cit., pp. 253–82; Lamb, *History*, pp. 459–78; H. Frei, *The Eclipse of Biblical Narrative* (New Haven: Yale Univ. Press, 1974); J. Walgrave, *Unfolding Revelation* (Philadelphia: Westminster, 1972), pp. 179–253.

26. Walgrave, pp. 135–78; G. McCool, *Catholic Theology in the Nineteenth Century* (New York: Seabury, 1977); W. Schulz, *Dogmenentwicklung als Problem der Geschichtlichkeit der Wahrheitserkenntnis* (Rome: Gregorian Univ. Press, 1969), pp. 71–124.

27. Cf. P. Barthel, *Interpretation du langage mythique et théologie biblique* (Leiden: Brill, 1963); W. Pannenberg, *Philosophy of Science and Theology* (Philadelphia: Westminster, 1976), pp. 29–224.

28. Cf. G. Picht, *Wahrheit, Vernunft, Verantwortung* (Stuttgart: 1969), pp. 108–40, 183–202, 281–407.

29. Cf. Lonergan, *Method*, pp. 253–93; Peukert, op. cit., pp. 250–323; E. Becker, *The Structure of Evil* (New York: Braziller, 1968).

30. Cf. Metz, "Erinnerung," *Handbuch phil. Grundbegriffe* (Munich: Kösel, 1973), vol. 2, pp. 386–98; idem, "The Future in the Memory of Suffering," *Concilium* 76 (1972): 9–25; Segundo, op. cit., pp. 175–81; Lonergan, *Method*, pp. 311–20.

31. Cf. Lonergan, *Grace and Freedom* (New York: Herder and Herder, 1971), pp. 80–92, 103–9; idem, *De Constitutione Christi On-*

*tologica et Psychologica* (Rome: Gregorian Univ. Press, 1961), pp. 51–56.

32. B. Lonergan, *The Way to Nicea* (Philadelphia: Westminster, 1976); idem, "The Origins of Christian Realism," in *A Second Collection* (Philadelphia: Westminster, 1974), pp. 239–61. Both these writings attempt to show how the development of doctrine was not simply the result of the impact of Graeco-Roman conceptuality upon Christianity. Cf. the following chapter for further discussion of this.

33. E. Peterson, "Der Monotheismus als politisches Problem und Christus als Imperator," in *Theologische Traktate* (Munich: Kösel, 1951), pp. 45–147, 150–64. Also the reference in n. 86 of chap. 5.

34. J. Segundo, *Our Idea of God* (Maryknoll: Orbis, 1974); F. Fiorenza, "Critical Social Theory and Christology," in *Catholic Theological Society of America Proceedings* 30 (1975): 63–110; J. B. Metz, *Followers of Christ* (New York: Paulist Press, 1978); S. Moore, *The Crucified Jesus Is No Stranger* (New York: Seabury, 1977); J. Shea, *Stories of God* (Chicago: Thomas More Press, 1977). Also Segundo Galilea, *Espiritualidad de la liberación* (Santiago: Ed. ISPLAJ, 1973); Geffré and Gutiérrez (eds.), *The Mystical and Political Dimension of Christian Faith* (New York: Herder and Herder, 1974); and John F. Kavanaugh, *Following Christ in a Consumer Society: The Spirituality of Cultural Resistance* (Maryknoll: Orbis Books, 1981).

# Chapter 5

# Orthopraxis and Theological Method

*Toward a Political Hermeneutics of Transcendental Theology*

**K**arl Rahner and Bernard Lonergan are two major figures in contemporary Catholic systematic theology. Within very different cultural contexts, and from very different perspectives, they have attempted to develop transcendental orientations in their respective theologies. A common assumption is that any theology done in self-critical solidarity with the victims of history would have to reject any transcendental orientation as too idealist. In my judgment such an assumption is profoundly mistaken. Victims struggle to transcend the injustice of their suffering. Transcendental orientations need not issue in idealist abstractions but can be an expression of those constitutive elements of practical reason as reason not yet realized in history and society. Without a dialectical appropriation of such a transcendental orientation, criticism can too easily slip into either empiricism or nihilism—as is evident in those interpretations of Marx which neglect his dialectical relationship with Hegel. If the ages of intellectual and religious innocence are past, then any theology concerned with the foundational importance of praxis should engage in a dialectical appropriation of transcendence, not as an exercise in idealist dreaming, but as a concrete orientation critical of social reality in its present alienated condition. Such a critical realist position moves decisively beyond the false alternatives of empiricism and idealism. It is realist inasmuch as it recognizes the inherent orientation of human beings to go beyond or transcend the injustices of their present situations. I analyzed this in terms of the transcendental projects of critical theory in chapter two. I showed how such a critical transcendental orientation is also one of the main differences between the second and fifth models of theologically relating theory and praxis in chapter three. The previous chapter sketched how a praxis enlightenment, cognizant of such a transcendental orientation, could undertake a socially critical reconstruction of church teachings. In this chapter I shall first outline the hermeneutics of suspicion and recovery which Metz uses to appropriate dialectically Rahner's transcendental theology. Then I shall indicate how Lonergan's transcendental orientation can effectively meet the issues raised by both the transcendental-idealist and the dialectical-materialist phases of the turn to concrete subjects in history. Finally, the relevance of Lonergan's work for themes associated with orthopraxis and theological method will be treated.

## A Dialectic of Suspicion and Recovery

On the basis of both Metz's lectures and his recent book, *Faith in History and Society,* I understand his political theology to be related dialectically to Karl Rahner's transcendental theology. The relation is dialectical inasmuch as Metz negates and affirms Rahner's theology. He negatively criticizes the transcendental-idealist conceptuality Rahner employs in formulating his theological positions, but Metz affirms the intellectual and spiritual performance out of which Rahner theologizes. Indeed, the negative criticisms are meant to emphasize that intellectual and spiritual performance by giving it a more concretely historical and narrative articulation. These negations and affirmations might be termed, to borrow the procedures of Paul Ricoeur, a hermeneutics of suspicion and a hermeneutics of recovery.

Disagreements are usually a function of the proximity of the divergent positions. More volumes than even Rahner himself has written would be needed to expound the intellectual and spiritual indebtedness of Metz to his mentor and close personal friend, Karl Rahner. Their disagreements arise from the different contexts to which they address their shared conviction that Catholic fundamental theology must effectively promote a critical questioning of contemporary cultures and societies from the perspective of the Christian faith and Catholic traditions; as well it must promote a critical questioning of traditional religious beliefs and institutionalized practices within Christianity and Catholicism from the perspective of the contradictions in contemporary cultures and societies. This shared conviction has led Metz, from 1966 to the present, to develop a new political theology which includes (among many other elements I cannot mention now) a hermeneutics of suspicion regarding Rahner's transcendental theology. At the risk of oversimplification, the following are some of the main criticisms of his political hermeneutics:

1. A suspicion that Rahner's transcendental theology is too dependent upon a metaphysical conceptuality derivative from the traditions of German idealism running from Kant's *Critique of Pure Reason* through the right-wing Hegelians to Heidegger and Maréchal;

2. A suspicion that such a metaphysical conceptuality, unable to thematize the concrete origins of ideas and concepts, too easily spills over into a somewhat romanticist idealization of originating, prethematic experience as unifying and unproblematic, thereby downplaying the concretely contradictory and problematic character of human experience in history and society;

3. A suspicion that this metaphysical fascination with ideas and an unproblematic originating experience does not provide strong enough foundations to criticize the fascination of instrumental rationality with technique and its cultural offspring, middle-class consumerism, since both fascinations neglect the concreteness of historical and social human subjects;

4. A suspicion that a fundamental theology formulated with such a metaphysical conceptuality would promote an idealized universality of humanity constituted in a preapprehension of God, paralleling an idealized universality of anonymous Christianity which, like the hedgehog in the German fable to which Metz refers in criticizing Rahner's transcendental conceptuality, would project the illusion of having won the race without having actually run.[1] Concepts do not move.

5. A suspicion, finally, exists that the theological foundations of Christian faith should not introduce us into the concept of Christianity so much as into an understanding of *both* the genuinely prereligious conflicts and questions (the identity crisis of becoming human subjects) to which the memory of Christian narratives responds, *and* the intellectual, moral, and religious imperatives of being doers of the Word as well as hearers of the Word (the identity crisis of becoming Christian subjects).

If I understand Metz correctly, this hermeneutics of suspicion regarding the metaphysical conceptuality of Rahner aims not simply at negating his transcendental theology but at actually *realizing* its intention of turning to the subject (anthropocentrism) concretely in our personal, social, and ecclesial practice. The hermeneutics of suspicion ground a hermeneutics of recovery.

Metz calls our attention to how the intellectual and spiritual performance of Rahner's theologizing breaks through the metaphysical conceptuality of transcendental idealism.[2] The hermeneutics of suspicion is concerned with distancing us from the conceptuality so that we might really experience the historical tensions of contemporary questioning intelligence thirsting for what no concept or idea could ever satiate. We are reminded of Marx's criticisms of Hegel. The political hermeneutics of suspicion seem more directed at us, the readers in front of the text, than at the performance of Rahner behind the text. Metz warns us that it would be a false and distorted reading of Rahner's work to view it as a calm conceptual unfolding from *Spirit in World* to the latest volume of the *Theological Investigations.* Rahner must not be left to some dry, academic history of ideas course. Metz will often call attention to the classic quality of Rahner's theology: "we can often find support for objections to his theories in the broader context of his own thinking." That broader context, I suggest, is the intellectual and spiritual performance of Rahner's theologizing. It is on this basis that a narrative and practical hermeneutics of recovery would read Rahner's transcendental theology, not as disclosive of an "always already" achieved Christian identity, but as imperatives impelling us toward personal and social transformations of a world "not yet" truly human and "not yet" truly Christlike. Without the hedge-hog the hare would not have run.

Among the many elements in Metz's political hermeneutics of recovery, I would like to single out three. First, in the essay on "Theology as Biography," Metz shows how Rahner introduced the concrete human subject into his reflections on doctrinal con-ceptuality. Rahner has taught us to read church doctrine as the expression of a praxis-grounded existential biography of the Christian community. What Rahner began for dogmatics, politi-cal theology would extend to the whole of theology. The latter must be grounded, not on concepts and ideas, but on the dynam-ics of historical and social human subjects striving to live out the call to conversion, *metanoia,* or exodus as intellectual, moral, so-cial, and religious imperatives. Here the recovery of political theology is very close to the transcendental method of Bernard Lonergan.

Second, as I already mentioned, political theology recovers the transcendental thrust by understanding it, not as disclosive of human being "always already" before God but as imperatives to transform ourselves and every human being into more atten-tive, intelligent, reasonable, responsible, and loving subjects— subjects, as Metz writes, who respond to the demands of their historical times and social experiences, seeking ever anew to re-alize truly human and Christlike identities in their world. Humans who realize that their presence to God calls them to be truly responsible human subjects.[3] The social sins of racism, sex-ism, ecological destruction, political and economic oppression cannot be adequately counteracted within the churches and so-ciety at large by pious or indignant moralisms, nor by cleverly conceived techniques. They require profound conversions of personal, social, cultural, economic, and political conduct or praxis. To argue, for example, that multinational corporations should continue collaborating with and supporting the apart-heid government in South Africa because this provides some jobs for some black South Africans can be a technique of evasion, a rationalization whereby we evade *our* responsibility because we thereby deny the majority of South Africans the ability to exercise for themselves *their* responsibility as truly human subjects. It overlooks the fact that South Africa is constitutionally the only state in the world legally based upon white supremacy.

Finally, a political hermeneutics recovers the concrete history of suffering through which Rahner theologized. Metz has reminded us that in reading Karl Rahner we are confronted more with the challenge of an abiding question than with the comfort of a complacent answer. Metz's own critical questioning of Rahner's transcendental theology should call our attention to the concrete historical context of Rahner's writings. Rahner loved the church enough to challenge official policies when those contradicted the demands of fidelity to the ongoing *traditio* or handing on of the faith. Nor was it in the cheap grace of romantic idealism that Rahner gained insight into how anthropocentrism is profoundly theocentric. That insight concretely emerged within the darkness and despair of a human and historical identity crisis, the apocalyptic dimensions of which can only be glimpsed in the many histories of suffering spread across two world wars. Only a mind and heart steeped in the mystery of the crucified would have had the audacity to think of humanity as "Spirit in World" and "Hearer of the Word" amidst the din and carnage of Germany in the late 1930s and 1940s. If the narrative folly of the cross confounds the so-called wisdom of this world (by some estimates almost half of all natural scientists in the First World are engaged in military-related research), we dare not imagine that the identity crisis of humanity etched in the holocaust of those years is now behind us. While millions of human beings go without sufficient food and shelter, the ovens of a thousand Auschwitzes are now neatly produced and packaged with all the cool "logic" of the nuclear arms race. Just as, in the words of Lonergan, "there are real theological problems, real issues that, if burked, threaten the very existence of Christianity," so there are real political problems, real issues that, if burked, threaten the very existence of humanity.[4] Metz's political theology, by showing how the identity crisis of Christianity is intimately related to the identity crisis of humanity, recovers critically the central insight of Rahner into the God-centeredness of human-centeredness in the dying and risen Christ.

### Praxis and Generalized Empirical Method

Some might argue that to assess the contributions of Lonergan and Rahner to the themes of concern to political theology is unduly to slant the discussion toward Kantian or Hegelian perspectives. After all, Marx's resounding call to praxis was precisely a critique of the transcendental and theoretical critiques of Kant and Hegel, while Rahner and Lonergan are transcendental Thomists and so rather removed from concerns with praxis. Such objections, however, fail to appreciate both the differing contributions of the two theologians and the project envisaged in Marx's call to praxis.

To begin with the latter, Marx's lifelong efforts to sublate philosophy into social praxis were by no means a complete negation of the transcendental projects associated with German idealism. If there are few issues on which the many divergent schools of Marxist scholarship agree, this would be one of them. Indeed, I would agree with Alvin Gouldner's assessment in his Marxist analysis of Marxism, and with others, that a basic element in the contradictions and anomalies imbedded in the development of Marxist theory and praxis can be traced to German idealist traditions.[5] As the young Marx stated with regard to Kant, and the mature Marx with regard to Hegel, the aim of his control of theory through social praxis was not to replace theories or ideas with some kind of mindless activism, but to understand idealists like Kant and Hegel as unknowingly and uncritically reflecting in their theories concrete social values and disvalues.[6] The modern "turn to the subject" initiated by Kant and German idealism is singularly important for an adequate understanding of contemporary efforts at elaborating a methodologically grounded praxis enlightenment.[7] The turn to the subject has two major phases: the transcendental-idealist phase (Kant, Hegel, right-wing Hegelians) and the dialectical-materialist phase (left-wing Hegelians, Marx, Marxists). Common to both these phases is a concern to promote the responsible freedom of humankind in the face of the increasing cognitive, social, and cultural domination of the natural sciences with the empirico-mathematical techniques of observation, verification, and industrial application.[8] Kant's critiques, especially the *Critique of Practical Rea-*

*son,* sought to protect the realm of moral praxis and freedom as a noumenal realm over against the phenomenal realm of necessity. Hegel recognized the inconsistency of this phenomenon-noumenon dichotomy and sought to develop a conceptualistic intellectual praxis aimed at sublating all meanings and values into the constitutive meaning of *Geist* as coherent and complete system.[9] The decisive discovery by Hegel of history as constituted by meaning—Lonergan once remarked to me that the initial expressions of this can be found in Hegel's early theological writings—was a heady experience indeed.

While the right-wing Hegelians attempted to maintain that the factual institutions of society in church and state incarnated constitutive reason, the left-wing Hegelians had, perhaps, drunk more deeply of the discovery and tended to follow Feuerbach's call for an absolute negation of existing historical and social institutions in order to recreate society and history in the anthropocentric image of a radically secularized constitutive rationality.[10] The turn to the subject passed from the transcendental-idealist phase, with its emphasis on moral praxis (freedom) and intellectual praxis (concept), to the dialectical-materialist phase. The young Hegelians promoted a historical praxis aimed at realizing concretely in history (or materially) constitutive rationality. The empirical methods of the natural sciences, as Feuerbach stated, once united to the new philosophy would collaborate in creating a new truth and a new freedom: autonomous secularized humankind.[11]

If Marx could write that "there is no other road for you to *truth* and *freedom* except that leading *through* the brook of fire (the Feuerbach),"[12] he soon recognized that the heady optimism of the young Hegelian emphasis on historical praxis aimed at meaning was neither dialectical nor concretely material enough. The turn to the subject would, for Marx, only be real and concrete insofar as a social, revolutionary praxis would aim at realizing the value of human life by transforming society from its capitalist alienated stage of production and social relations of domination to a socialist stage of freely associated producers.

As Professor O'Malley and others have indicated, Marx's materialist conception of society and history (Marx never wrote of "dialectical materialism") aimed at fusing natural science and dialectical criticism by materially inverting Hegel's discussion of the ethical life in *The Philosophy of Right*.[13] If social praxis aims at a unity of theory and praxis in terms of concrete human values, then Marx was convinced that simple-minded moralisms against greedy capitalists were just so much nonsense. Ignorance of infrastructural value-conflicts rather than greed was at fault. Marx envisaged a massive empirical-dialectical study of economic values as the concrete embodiment of Hegel's abstract ideas. The conceptions of Hegel's discussion of civil society would be materialized in Marx's analysis of capital, landed property, wage labor. Hegel's conceptions of state constitution would be materialized in a treatment of economic activity of the state. Hegel's ideas on international law would materialize in Marx's analysis of international trade. And, finally, world history would be concretized in terms of an analysis of the world market.[14] Marx never lived to complete even the first part of the first part (*Capital*) of this ambitious project. He was constantly revising his dialectical analyses in the light of ever new empirical studies which, as the correspondence over the last thirty years of his life attests, were simply too many for any one person to keep up with.[15]

The purpose of this quick overview of the turn to the subject in its transcendental-idealist and dialectical-materialist phases is twofold.

First, it intimates an abiding, deep-rooted dichotomy between the determinism increasingly operative in eighteenth- and nineteenth-century empirical natural sciences and the concerns of these philosophers of praxis for human freedom. As Alvin Gouldner amply demonstrates in *The Two Marxisms*, the anomalies in Marx's development itself (e.g., materialist conception of history; the infrastructure as juxtaposing both the forces and relations of production; the necessary empirically analyzable laws of capitalism would inevitably lead to its own breakdown and replacement by socialism versus the need to organize the revolutionary cadres to overthrow capitalism) have not been resolved in the subsequent history of Marxism. We are still confronted in theory and praxis with the two poles of Scientific Marxism (determinism, object-oriented) and Critical Marxism (voluntaristic, subject-oriented); for example, Lenin-Stalin versus Trotsky-Gramsci, Structuralist Marxism versus the Frankfurt School.[16]

Nor is this rift only troublesome for Marxists. In philosophy there are trends either to erect the logical techniques of the natural sciences into the canon for all valid knowledge (e.g., positivism, naturalism, logicism, linguistic analysis of the Vienna circle, historicism, structuralism) or to preserve some domain for freedom which could not be invaded by the sciences (e.g., idealism, some forms of phenomenology, existentialism, personalism).[17] Human sciences such as psychology and sociology are marked by similar dichotomies, e.g., behaviorism versus humanism, functionalism versus symbolic interactionism, and most recently sociobiologism versus anthropologism.[18] Nor are theologians immune from all this, as is all too evident in the tensions between religious studies and theology, between historical-critical exegesis and doctrinal systematics.[19]

Second, I believe the *philosophical* contributions of Rahner and Lonergan can be differentiated according to how each of them directed his own retrieval of Aquinas toward overcoming the dichotomy from differing perspectives. Rahner's cognitional metaphysics in *Geist in Welt* essayed a quasi-Heideggerian transcendental retrieval of Aquinas. It attempted an ontological mediation of primordially originating experience and conceptualization through an *existential* thematization of the prior unthematic *existentiell* of transcending experience. Against Kant, Rahner held that the "ought" of moral and metaphysical principles is not beyond the range of human experience; against Hegel, he affirmed the unity-in-difference of reality and ideality to be in prethematic experience open to the transcendent rather than in conceptualization per se.[20] If from Aquinas Rahner saw the inexhaustible ground and goal of all questioning in God as mystery, and from Heidegger how the question is the piety of thought, then it is little wonder that his achievements were to roam over the manifold questions confronting Christianity and Catholicism seeking to shift the *status quaestionis* from the ontic categories of a cosmological metaphysics to the ontological categories of cognitive metaphysics.[21] Where Rahner's transcendental turn to the subject essayed a creative Catholic response to, and critical appropriation of, the transcendental-idealist phase, Johann B. Metz's political theology has attempted to articulate a foundational theology appropriate for those questions and challenges posed by the dialectical-materialist phase of the turn to the subject.[22] While the originating primordial experience as openness to mystery through the *Woraufhin* of human questing is indeed a foundational orientation of human experience, still for Metz Rahner has paid too little attention both to the problematic character of human experience, especially in its intrinsically social and historical dialectical dimensions, and may have conceded too much to the conceptional-ideational aspects of transcendental-idealist traditions in dealing with the many disputed questions in theology.[23] For Metz, Rahner's achievements must be complemented by critical collaboration with the natural and human sciences; they must be explicitly related to the concrete histories of suffering associated with the struggles for liberation and redemption.[24]

Lonergan's retrieval of Aquinas, on the other hand, was not in terms of a cognitional metaphysics but rather a theoretical articulation of cognitive praxis or performance underlying both the transitions from consciousness to knowledge and from knowledge to action.[25] Instead of moving away from the empirical sciences toward an ontological refuge of human freedom and self-determination, Lonergan proceeded to uncover the dynamic and heuristic performance of questioning as grounding all advances in empirically scientific knowing.[26] From this he dialectically challenged the notions of deterministic necessity and axiomatic deductivism, which not only misled so many articulations of empirical science but also alienated social and cultural living. They did this by attempting to impose conceptual necessities through the use of technocratic and bureaucratic techniques.[27] If Lonergan learned from Aquinas that proportionate being as the concrete universal is shot through with contingency, he creatively transposed those insights in terms of a complementarity of classical and statistical procedures in empirical science. These yielded, not a universe whose laws could be theoretically deduced according to some iron necessity, but a

universe of emergent probability open to the rhythms of limita-
tion and transcendence, and constitutive of the dialectical tensions between essential and effective human freedom.[28] Lonergan's work through *Insight* is a massive transposition of the basic
presuppositions underlying the transcendental-idealist phase of
the turn to the subject. The Kantian dichotomy between phenomenal necessity (known by the empirical sciences) and noumenal freedom (oriented to moral praxis) is overcome by adverting to the actually related and recurrent performance of
what we do when we know.[29] Such attention to cognitive praxis
discloses the alienations operative in believing that we know the
real through sensitive intuition (*sinnliche Anschauung*). If
knowing is not taking a good look but verifying insights into
sensible and imaginative data, then moral praxis is not volun-
taristically following the categorical imperatives encapsulated
in noumenal subjectivity. Rather, moral praxis positively sublates the underlying sensitive flow of desires and fears, through
practical insight and evaluative reflection, to reach decisions on
contingent courses of action whereby we can extend the range of
effective human freedom.[30]

The Hegelian shift from sensitive to intellectual intuition (*in-
tellektuelle Anschauung*) with its orientation toward a conceptualistic intellectual praxis dominated by knowledge and theory
is replaced in Lonergan by an attunement to the related and recurrent operations of conscious intentionality. This shifts attention from logic to method and acknowledges the coherent but
radically incomplete (and so ongoing) character of the human
spirit's (*Geist*) quest for meaning and value.[31] The problematic
ambiguity of concrete human experiences in history cannot,
Lonergan reminds us, be overcome by the equally problematic
ambiguity of abstract human knowledge in history.[32] The metaphysical logic of an Hegelian type, presupposing as it does
an eventual completeness of system and theory, cannot be
*die Gesamt- und Grundwissenschaft*. Lonergan's transcendental
method strives for coherence but frankly admits its radical in-
completeness. The operations of conscious intentionality are indeed both factual ("is") and normative ("ought"). Yet this fusion
of the factual and the normative is not the indicative ("always

already") possession of *Geist* within the world of theory but is the imperative ("not yet') beckoning of concrete human strivings toward attentiveness, intelligence, reasonableness, and responsible love.[33] The fusion is a project, not a possession. The foundations of intellectual praxis in transcendental method are not some set of theories, however brilliant, but questioning human beings living within the multiple and changing patterns of natural and historical processes.[34] Idealism, as Lonergan mentions, is only a halfway house between empiricism and such a critical realism.[35]

If Lonergan's early work can be seen as transposing the basic presuppositions of the transcendental-idealist phase, then I believe his later work (from *Method in Theology* to his present work in macroeconomics) can be viewed as a creative and critical response to the challenge of the dialectical-materialist phase of the turn toward the subject.

In *Method in Theology* Lonergan indicates the pressing need for dialectical criticism to inform historical and social praxis.

> There are the deviations occasioned by neurotic need. There are the refusals to keep on taking the plunge from settled routine to an as yet unexperienced but richer mode of living. There are the mistaken endeavors to quiet an uneasy conscience by ignoring, belittling, denying, rejecting higher values. Preference scales become distorted. Feelings soured. Bias creeps into one's outlook, rationalization into one's morals, ideology into one's thoughts. So one may come to hate the truly good and love the really evil. Nor is that calamity limited to individuals. It can happen to groups, to nations, to blocks of nations, to mankind. It can take different, opposed, belligerent forms to divide mankind and to menace civilization with destruction. Such is the monster that has stood forth in our day.[36]

The monster of contemporary alienation intimates how the age of innocent criticism, i.e., criticism innocent of its own presuppositions, has begun to end. As Lonergan later wrote, "the more human studies turn away from abstract universals and attend to concrete human beings, the more evident it becomes that the scientific age of innocence has come to an end: human authenticity can no longer be taken for granted. . . . It is only after the age of innocence that praxis becomes an academic subject."[37] Empirical human sciences are not sufficiently objective to the degree that they ignore the complex dialectics of decline in which (1) "the data may be a mixed product of authenticity and unauthenticity," and (2) "the very investigation of the data may be affected by the personal or inherited unauthenticity of the investigators."[38]

With increasing frequency over the last six years, Lonergan has referred to his work not as "transcendental method" but as "generalized empirical method." His empirical method is "generalized" in two radical ways: (1) it attends to both the data of sense and the data of consciousness; and (2) the data of consciousness involve not only a genetically related series of sublations from data through understanding and judgment to decision and action but also the need for an ongoing series of dialectically operative methods which are grounded in decisions and actions aimed at promoting good and overcoming alienation.[39] The dialectically operative methods are what Lonergan terms "method as praxis." Where empirical methods move from experiential data, through ranges of understanding relative to the data, and through judgments discerning whether such understandings are correct or not to decisions and actions, method-as-praxis has a reverse orientation. It seeks to explicate the value commitments, or value conflicts operative in decisions and actions. People respond to value in actions embodying love or hate even though they cannot explain fully to what they are responding. The knowledge flows from the loving or hating actions; and it flows in terms of judgments of value or disvalue wherein they judge concrete situations in the light of the values they love, and the disvalues they hate. From such judgments they engage in what Ricoeur calls a hermeneutics of recovery (regarding values) and a hermeneutics of suspicion (regarding disvalues) on the level of understanding. Finally, from such decisions, judgments, and hermeneutics, they engage in an empirically transformative action which changes both the data of sense and the data of consciousness, which in turn changes both human hearts and human social and cultural institutions.[40]

Although one could claim that all of Lonergan's work in method is praxis in so far as it is concerned with the question of what we *do* when we know, still Lonergan himself also acknowledges a more transformative sense of praxis in which decision and action precede and ground a knowledge of values, lead to understandings which engage in a hermeneutics of suspicion as well as of recovery, and thereby engages in a transformation not only of the data of sense but also the data of consciousness itself.[41]

Now such a generalized empirical method, with its attention to dialectics and praxis, critically responds to the concerns of the dialectical-materialist phase of the turn toward the subject. With the young Hegelians it acknowledges the centrality of constitutive meaning in historical praxis. History is constituted by human meanings and values which not only grow and flourish but also disintegrate and decay. While the self-appropriation that is foundational to generalized empirical method is intensely personal, it is not private or monadic. Quite the contrary. Such self-appropriation is intrinsically related (as all persons are) to the ongoing history of humankind itself.[42] Thus Lonergan can write that generalized empirical method is indeed experimental. "But the experiment is conducted not by any individual, not by any generation, but by the historical process itself."[43] Unlike the young Hegelians, however, our twentieth century has profoundly shaken secularist faith in humankind's ability to carry off the experiment on its own. In an unpublished essay of 1974 on "Sacralization and Secularization," Lonergan indicates how the undifferentiated sacralism of the Middle Ages led from the seventeenth century onward to a defensive clerical sacralism in Roman Catholicism which tended to extend "the mantle of religion over the opinions of ignorant men."[44] Such an undifferentiated and defensive sacralism provoked, especially from the nineteenth century onwards, an equally undifferentiated and offensive secularism. We have witnessed, as Max Weber intimates, the alienating transition from a hierarchic *sacralist* authoritarianism to a bureaucratic *secularist* authoritarianism.[45]

Like all authoritarianisms, the two tend to reinforce one another over the heads of people and communities. The illusion of a god identical with ecclesial-social institutions is not radically different from the illusion of a humankind identical with political-economic institutions.[46] The need of our times is for a differentiation of sacred and secular attuned to the genuine and the pathological in both. Lonergan's reflections on the structure of the human good and the dialectic of religious experience will be helpful in such a task of differentiation.[47]

The creative and critical responses to the ongoing challenges of Marxist social theory and praxis by generalized empirical method are extensive and deeply transformative. I have already referred to Alvin Gouldner's *The Two Marxisms* which traces the origins and development of the contradictions and anomalies between Scientific Marxism and Critical Marxism. The former is characterized by an empirical determinism convinced that necessary laws of social development would, irrespective of human freedom, lead to the demise of capitalism. The objective creates the subjective. Critical Marxism, on the other hand, is characterized by a dialectical voluntarism convinced of the need to instill a revolutionary messianism in peoples in order to change existing social structures. The subjective creates the objective.[48] Gouldner sees these two Marxisms as two extremes, both present in Marx, and defining (as ideal-types) the ends of a continuum between one or the other pole of which all subsequent Marxist theory and praxis has vacillated.[49] Nor is he alone in such a formulation; he points to similar studies by Karl Korsch, Lucio Colletti, Merleau-Ponty, Mihailo Markovic, Dick Howard, Karl Klare, Eric Hobsbawn, and Perry Anderson.[50]

Generalized empirical method exposes the cognitive and epistemological misunderstanding regarding so-called necessary deterministic laws in nature and history by its articulation of concrete cognitive performance and its attendant emergent probability. It also maps out the interlocking mediations of empirical and dialectical methods capable of radically displacing the dichotomies of scientistic determinism and voluntaristic decisionism.[51] In place of these alienated and alienating dichotomies, generalized empirical method elaborates an ongoing complementarity of empirical methods (classical, statistical, genetic) and dialectical methods in which the results of empirical investigations provide the data for a dialectical discernment of the values and disvalues they exhibit.[52] The dialectically foundational articulation of genuinely humanizing praxis promotes a value critique, and systematic understandings of the ramifications of values and disvalues, in order to transform the social situations from which empirical human sciences in turn draw their data.[53] This, in very abbreviated fashion, is the metascientific theory-praxis mediation based on Lonergan's functional specialties which I have developed in *History, Method and Theology.*[54]

Moreover, this is not only relevant to the dichotomy within Marxist social praxis and theory but also to analogous dichotomies that bedevil both philosophy in general and scientific methodologies.[55]

In a letter to Walter Benjamin, Theodor Adorno wrote in 1935: "A restoration of theology, or better, a radicalization of the dialectic into the very glowing core of theology, would at the same time have to mean an utmost intensification of the social-dialectical, indeed economic, motifs."[56]

During the past few years Lonergan has taken up again the work in macroeconomics he began during the 1930s. To those skeptical of self-educated economists, I would recall how neither Adam Smith nor Karl Marx, nor, for that matter, many of the key figures in Schumpeter's massive *A History of Economic Analysis,* had doctorates in economics. If Marx's concern with social praxis was guided by a concrete understanding of value as at bottom economic value, then Lonergan has understood how a genuinely dialectical critique of Marxist materialism should meet head-on the problem of massive economic oppression and exploitation that materialist dialectic sought to remedy.[57] Marx tried to discern criteria for economic progress or decline immanent in the economic infrastructure constituted by the industrializing forces and relations (the human relations to nature and to other human beings) of production. In a critically similar manner, Lonergan's macroeconomics connects his dialectic of the observance or nonobservance of the transformative transcendental imperatives (be attentive, be intelligent, be reasonable, be responsible, be loving) with his macroeconomic analysis. His *Circulation Analysis* tries to discern the criteria immanent in production processes with their alternating stages of surplus expansions and basic expansions. "But the dialectic arises from the contradiction that arises when the criteria are adverted to or not, understood or not, affirmed or denied, observed responsibly or disregarded, by a community of love or a community of egoists."[58]

Contemporary Catholic social teaching has continually criticized the alienating shortcomings of both late capitalism and state socialism. But, as liberation theologians are quick to point out, if these criticisms, however justified in themselves, are not to degenerate into a value-neutral legitimation of the status quo, then we must elaborate an accurate and critical economic theory and praxis capable of concretely and dialectically overcoming the alienation so massively present in both.[59] Moralistic appeals to the common good, subsidiarity, and the just wage are hardly sufficient. As I have argued elsewhere, Lonergan's macroeconomics is as insightfully challenging in its potential contributions to really humanizing economic processes, as his earlier work in method is in regard to basic cognitive issues. The latter offers us a way to unmask the myriad forms of empiricism and idealism, not as opposites but as different aspects of a radical neglect of transformative cognitive praxis; his macroeconomics will help us to understand how the many forms of late capitalism and state socialism are the alienated and alienating results of a deep-seated ignorance of the criteria constitutive of the alternating basic and surplus stages of the production process. To repeat, late capitalism is a bad materialization of idealism, whereas state socialism is a bad idealization of materialism.[60] What humankind doesn't know has hurt it, for this ignorance continues to spawn the economic misadventures (as Lonergan terms them) of colonialism, welfarism, and multinationalism.[61] Such are the economic monstrosities which have stood forth in our day generating widespread poverty, unemployment, inflations, recessions, militarisms, depressions. The terribly dehumanizing effects can be read all too easily in the sufferings of millions of human beings.[62]

## Orthopraxis and Theological Method

Within the above context I have presented some of the main critical contributions which Lonergan's generalized empirical method has made to the theme of praxis in the turn to the subject with its transcendental-idealist and dialectical-materialist phases. I concentrated more on the German philosophical context of that turn in order to highlight the similarities and differences between him and Rahner. Where Rahner's creative contributions have been directed more at a transposition of the issues raised by the transcendental-idealist phase, Lonergan has essayed a transposition as well of the issues raised by the dialectical-materialist phase. As a result, Lonergan's articulation of generalized empirical method seems to be especially helpful in sorting out the many methodological misunderstandings that haunt not only philosophy in general, and the philosophies of praxis in particular, but also the human sciences and scholarship.

In the light of these contributions one can, perhaps, appreciate why Lonergan can bluntly write that "orthopraxy has a value beyond orthodoxy" and that the profound change in the structures and procedures of theology articulated in method "places orthopraxis above orthodoxy."[63] Orthopraxis in this sense has, I believe, two meanings. Its primary meaning refers to the genuine practice of religion whereby humans appropriate the religious meanings and values transmitted by their religious tradition. In this primary sense, then, orthodoxies can be expressions of the orthopraxis of religious communities at particular places and times. This primary orthopraxis is the concrete realization in history of religious conversion as an ongoing withdrawal from sinful hate and indifference.[64] As genuine (or ortho-) praxis, it can never be simply taken for granted or automatically guaranteed in any religious tradition. It is the fruit of God's grace and free, human, communal response. Such orthopraxis is foundational to the ongoing religious traditions in history.[65]

A second meaning of orthopraxis might be termed reflective, dialectical orthopraxis. This second meaning moves orthopraxis from its conscious primary meaning to a known and explicit thematization in order to aid theology in a move toward the "third stage of meaning" marked by the modern emergence of historical consciousness and the contemporary emergence of dialectical consciousness.[66] Lonergan sketches the relationship between these two meanings of orthopraxis when he writes:

> For religious communities are historical realities. Their authenticity is the resultant not only of the authenticity of their contemporary members but also of the heritage transmitted down the centuries. Whatever the defects of any such heritage, it comes to be accepted in good faith. Good faith is good, not evil. It needs to be purified, but the purification will be the slow product of historical research into the screening memories and defence mechanisms and legitimations that betray an original waywardness and a sinister turn.[67]

Lonergan sees both religious studies and theology challenged by a contemporary need to develop dialectical and critically practical methods for discerning genuine from alienated aspects in the historical realizations of religious traditions. Based upon his own work on the relationships between intellectual and religious conversions, Lonergan views the orientations of religious studies and theology as heading toward an overlapping and interchangeability. A reflectively dialectical orthopraxis calls for a creative openness to a "whole battery of methods" which, to the extent that they are operative in both religious studies and theology, will lead both sets of disciplines toward overlapping and interchangeability.[68]

This reflective, dialectical orthopraxis is "method as praxis." Lonergan writes of it:

> it discerns a radically distorted situation; it retreats from spontaneous to critical intelligence; it begins from above on the level of evaluations and decisions; and it moves from concord and cooperation towards the development of mutual understanding and more effective communications.[69]

The radical oppositions which distort the global situations of humankind mean that both religious studies and theology must "undertake dialectic, a dialectic that will asssemble all the dialectics that relate religions to organized secularism, religions to

one another, and the differing theologies that interpret the same
religious communion."[70]

Illustrative of such a dialectics now emerging in Christian
theologies are the conflicts in interpretation between historical-
critical and social-critical orientations toward past traditions.
The conflicts between conservative orthodoxy (which might
more accurately be termed "palaeodoxy") and liberal or mod-
ernist theologies in the early part of this century could be traced
to a common (mis)understanding of revelation. Orthodoxy was
viewed principally as affirmations of certain revealed factual
truths demanding intellectual assent. These were times when, in
Lonergan's phrase, "contemplative intellect, or speculative reason, or rigorous science were supreme, and practical issues were
secondary."[71] Conservatives appealed to a contemplative or
speculative pure reason which would assent to revealed, a-his-
torical facts or dogmas. Liberals rejected the latter in favor of
reading scripture as essentially reducible to secular moral
values.[72] Liberal historians developed historical-critical techniques which prescinded from the faith (or lack thereof) of the
exegete and/or historian. These techniques appealed to rigorous
science or scholarship which sought to disclose how religious
texts and orthodoxies were primarily expressions of the plausibility structures of the cultures or societies in which the text
emerged. Hence we had the theme of liberal historical criticism
on the "hellenization of Christianity" during the patristic and
conciliar periods.[73]

As Quentin Quesnell has observed, this factual orientation toward revelation, with is consequent reduction of values to secular moral values (à la neo-Kantians like Ritschl), tended to overlook the rather massive evidence in the scriptures of a revelation
of values transformative of the conduct of the believing communities.[74] In line with this shift, exegetes and historians are now
developing social-critical methods which interpret religious
texts and doctrines, not as merely reflecting the plausibility
structures of the cultures in which they emerged, but more importantly as criticizing those very plausibility structures. For example, there is Norman Gottwald's *The Tribes of Yahweh* or
Gerd Theissen's *Urchristliche Wundergeschichten,* Phyllis Tri-

ble's *God and the Rhetoric of Sexuality* or Richard Cassidy's *Jesus, Politics and Society* or Ben Meyer's *The Aims of Jesus.*[75] These are all very different exegetical and historical works; they raise many methodological issues which will be disputed and discussed for some time. In common, however, are their various critiques of, and corrections to, the presuppositions of liberal historical criticism. They refuse, in various manners, to interpret texts as doing no more than mirroring the plausibility structures and values of the surrounding cultures; instead they indicate the value conflicts expressed in the texts.[76]

Dialectics move beyond the aims of historical reconstruction. A reflectively dialectical orthopraxis takes seriously the need to thematize value conflicts within the heuristic of discerning values and disvalues, which is capable of distinguishing genuine historical progress toward freedom and humanization from dehumanizing decline. Dialectics, therefore, have to thematize horizons and breakdowns in terms of ongoing heuristics of histories and societies. William Loewe has shown how Lonergan's soteriology based upon the law of the cross is integrated within his philosophy of history with its practical intent.[77] Just as generalized empirical method is an experiment carried on with the historical process itself, so is this method far from being value-neutral with regard to psychic, moral, social, intellectual, and religious values and disvalues.

Take for instance Lonergan's outlines of dialectical analysis in his "The Origins of Christian Realism" and *The Way to Nicea.*[78] These studies are concerned with a dialectical analysis of intellectual value conflicts. Lonergan is interested neither in historical reconstructions of what the Fathers wrote nor in providing fresh data on past historical events. Rather his dialectics is based upon the intellectual appropriation of the cognitive dimensions of orthopraxis, aiming to discern how the values and disvalues which such an appropriation uncovers are present in the pre-Nicean movements. He is quite explicit that the Fathers "did not intend or desire" the intellectual value conflict he is analyzing.[79] He traces the conflict of values from Tertullian's naive empiricism, through Origen's Middle Platonist idealism, to Athanasius's hesitant affirmations of the critical realism of the Christian kerygma. While none of the Fathers in question explicitly knew or intended this conflict, it is one which underlies the ongoing differentiations of consciousness in human history.[80] Lonergan's dialectic analysis takes a critically grounded stand on the transformative values of: Be Attentive, Be Intelligent, Be Reasonable, Be Responsible, Be Loving. From that stand within intellectual or noetic orthopraxis, it moves on to judgments of value and of disvalue, and to a hermeneutics of suspicion regarding the disvalues of neglecting or truncating those transformative values, as well as to a hermeneutics of recovery regarding the instances where those values found concrete expression.

What Lonergan's brief analysis offers is, in his words, "a dialectic that, like an X-ray, sets certain key issues in high relief to concentrate on their oppositions and interplay."[81] Now, an X-ray is certainly no substitute for a full color picture. Patristic scholars who have labored long on research, interpretation, and historical reconstructions of the period in question, delicately assembling all the hues and tones of an author or event, could be shocked and disappointed at Lonergan's X-ray—especially if they had hardly a clue as to the values in conflict the X-ray highlights.[82] But X-rays are extremely useful in knowingly discerning pathological aberrations from genuine developments provided the practitioners know what to attend to. In Rosemary Haughton's phrase, "the present researches the past for the sake of the future."[83] Where historical-critical methods tend to move from empirical research through exegetical interpretations to historical reconstructions, those social-critical methods which are dialectical tend to move in an opposite direction. They articulate the basic values informing their commitments, and then move, through judgments of value and disvalue relative to those commitments, to a hermeneutics of recovery and a hermeneutics of suspicion regarding the values and disvalues in the traditions. Social-critical methods have as their goal the promotion of actions which will foster the values informing their basic commitments. To the degree that those values promote genuine self-transcendence, such social-critical methods are emergent realizations of what Lonergan terms "method as praxis," or what I have called a reflectively dialectical orthopraxis.

It would extend far beyond the scope of this study to analyze the many instances of social-critical methods now emerging in theology. There is an increasing debate among exegetes and theologians concerning the social-critical analyses of scripture and doctrine on the part of political and liberation theologians.[84] In political theology there are the differences between Metz's social-critical dialectics (aimed at moving from both conservative, paternalistic, and liberal, middle-class forms of church to the liberating, basic community form of church) and Hans Küng's historical-critical reconstructions aimed at liberal, democratic reforms of the church.[85] There are also the debates among patristic scholars and theologians relative to Erik Peterson's studies on monotheism as a political problem and the Trinitarian and Christological doctrines as expressions of a spirituality and revelatory transformation of values at odds with Roman political religion.[86] Critics of Latin American liberation theologies claim that the latter fail to observe the distinctions between witness and rigorous reflection, thereby slipping into types of ideological advocacy.[87] Those who argue theologically for the full incorporation of women into the ministries of the church are sometimes criticized for slighting the symbolism of sacramental traditions.[88]

While not entering into these and other debates, I would ask to what extent various forms of political and liberation theologies are committed to values neglected in other theologies, to what extent they are calling attention by their hermeneutics of suspicion and of recovery to "the screening memories and defense mechanisms and legitimations that betray an original waywardness and a sinister turn." The criticisms of their projects which appeal to historical-critical methods might themselves be unaware of the dialectical presuppositions of their own supposed scholarship and the need for a social-critical dialectics of historical criticism itself.[89] The contributions of Lonergan to orthopraxis and theological methods, in my judgment, indicate the importance of complementing and correcting the historical-critical methods by engaging in the development of dialectical, foundational, and critically practical methods attuned to the transformation of values revealed in biblical narratives and the

praxis of religious conversion. To the degree that the scriptures
and church doctrines expressed genuine (ortho-) religious praxis
of communities in the process of conversion or *metanoia* as an
ongoing withdrawal from dehumanizing and depersonalizing
sin, to that degree we need today a reflectively dialectical
orthopraxis methodologically capable of articulating the dialectic of values and disvalues unknown but consciously operative in
scriptural and doctrinal orthodoxies. Lonergan once remarked
that faith is indeed a leap, but not a leap into irrationality; faith
is a leap into reason away from the biased irrationalities of dehumanizing and depersonalizing social and historical bias. The
emergence of practical reason as reason yet to be realized in history—an emergence which can be read in the critiques of economic exploitation, racism, sexism, militarism—should be re-
trieved theologically by showing how religious faith, hope, and
love are constitutive elements of this reason not yet realized in
human social living.[90]

An important aspect of this retrieval involves the positive
sublation of church doctrines or orthodoxy in a reflectively dialectical orthopraxis. It is within the functional specialty of doctrines that Lonergan analyzes the ongoing discovery of mind or
reason in history. Doctrines are judgments of truth and falsity, of
value and disvalue, heuristically anticipating the reign of God
redemptively transforming human history. For "the intelligibility proper to developing doctrines is the intelligibility immanent
in historical process. One knows it, not by a priori theorizing,
but by a posteriori research, interpretation, history, dialectic,
and the decision of foundations."[91] For Lonergan, discerning
doctrinal development is discerning the transformatively religious judgments constitutive of practical reason as reason yet to
be realized in history. By way of an all too brief illustration, the
intellectual values and disvalues Lonergan has dialectically analyzed in the pre-Nicean movement can be correlated with the
sociopolitical values and disvalues Erik Peterson has analyzed in
his "Monotheismus als politisches Problem," and the sociosexual
values and disvalues Elizabeth S. Fiorenza has initially discerned
in "Early Christian History in a Feminist Perspective."[92] Naive
empiricism or materialism and idealism are not just vague ab-

stractions. As disvalues influencing cultural attitudes and social living, they alienate human beings and destroy effective personal and social freedom.

From the perspective of orthopraxis the real problems within Christianity today are not the result of real distinctions between natures and persons expressed in traditional orthodoxy. The real problems result from a failure of Christians to pay the cost of discipleship (Bonhoeffer) or the price of orthodoxy (Metz). That is, the real problems result from failures to sublate orthodoxy in an orthopraxis commensurate with the dialectics of values unknown but consciously operative in orthodoxy. How different, for instance, would the history of Christianity have been if Christians more genuinely lived the religious values expressed in the Trinitarian and Christological creeds. At a time when political and cultural forces were bent upon deforming Christianity into just another form of Roman imperial religion with a monistic monarchical one god, one emperor, one world, one religion, Nicea affirmed how God is a Trinitarian community of persons. Instead of hellenizing Christianity such credal confessions expressed a spirituality and a call for *metanoia* at odds with the plausibility structures and disvalues of the *Imperium Romanum*.[93] But how genuinely was this orthodoxy lived?

Analogously, today, I would argue that the real problems liberation theologies uncover in the disvalues of class oppression, racism, and sexism do not stem from the traditional distinctions between natures and person in Christ, nor are those disvalues reinforced by such distinctions. The exploitations of class, race, and sex within Christianity have resulted rather from failures to live up to the orthopraxis expressed in Christological orthodoxy. For the critical realist, distinctions between nature and personhood are capable of exposing the alienations resulting from the illusory opposites of naively empiricist forms of dualism and idealist forms of monism. The revelatory transformation of values narratively communicated in, e.g., chapter twenty-five of the Gospel of Matthew is indicative of the critical realism of the Christian kerygmata.[94] Similarly, as I have attempted to show elsewhere, the ecological plundering of nature now going on in industrialized societies is hardly a consequence of Judaeo-Christian values (*pace* Lynn White); rather it results from forms of naive empiricism and idealism rampant in secularist social and economic policies and practices from the nineteenth century down to our own day.[95] I have mentioned these issues in order to indicate how, in the framework of Lonergan's generalized empirical method, the dialectical methods needed for a reflective orthopraxis aim at knowingly realizing the transformative value orientations which are unknown but consciously operative in orthodoxy.

## Conclusions

Michael O'Callaghan's essay, "Rahner and Lonergan on Foundational Theology," supports my position on the fundamental similarities between the two Jesuit theologians regarding the foundational primacy of spontaneous religious orthopraxis as an ongoing response to God as loving mystery.[96] Yet there are differences. Although Rahner's "first level of reflection" and its "transcendental experience" have important analogues in Lonergan's "differentiation between consciousness and knowledge," nevertheless, Lonergan offers ways to verify the differentiation through a *public* process of self-appropriation. Thus Lonergan has articulated a *generalized* empirical method applicable not only to theology but to whole series of basic issues in the sciences and scholarly disciplines. Rahner's first level of reflection tends to concentrate upon formulating specifically Christian (and indeed, specifically Roman Catholic) theological categories. Thus many find his works more helpful in their own efforts to articulate the special foundational categories relevant to religious conversion and spirituality. Rahner is preeminently a mystagogic theologian. On the other hand, those interested in more general theological categories, i.e., categories operative not only in theologizing on the Christian mysteries but also operative in the sciences and other forms of noetic praxis, often find Lonergan's works more helpful. Lonergan is preeminently a methodological theologian. His life-long work has transformed method from its empiricist and idealist reifications as sets of axioms, principles, or systems into its concrete embodiments in the related and recurrent activities of ongoing communities of knowers and doers in history. Because of this, Lonergan cannot be accused of trying to immunize theology from critical human sciences and studies. Rahner leaves the intrinsic relationships between his first and second levels of reflection rather vague, to say the least.[97] Lonergan has initiated a framework for a reflectively dialectical orthopraxis critically open to the ongoing procedures and results of empirical and dialectical human sciences and scholarly disciplines. The intrinsic relationships between religious conversion processes and intellectual conversion processes which he has articulated challenge us to work out the constitutive interchangeability and overlapping of praxis as practical reason yet to be realized in history and the transcendental imperatives of human questing and questioning for the divine.

Lonergan's contextualization of orthopraxis and theological method within his work on generalized empirical method and macroeconomics is especially relevant in overcoming the long range problems and basic alienations which are at the root of the sufferings and victimizations to which various political and liberation theologies seek to respond. Karl Jaspers once observed: "For more than a hundred years it has been gradually realized that the history of scores of centuries is drawing to a close."[98] That aptly describes the epochal implications of the turn to the subject which, while it holds the promise of an ever fuller humanization and personalization of life on this planet, is also fraught—as any epochal transition is—with the risks and dangers of refusing to meet the challenges to intelligence, to love, and to freedom which such a turn demands. Neither reflection on theology nor reflection on method are ends in themselves. They are meant to promote a creative and critical collaboration with all humans in the tasks of transforming ourselves and our world into more attentive, intelligent, reasonable, and responsibly loving life. And, as Christians, we are called to incarnate our struggles for humanization and personalization in the transformative values of doing the truth in love revealed in the life, death, and resurrection of Jesus Christ.

## NOTES

1. Cf. Johann B. Metz, *Faith in History and Society* trans. David Smith (New York: Crossroad, 1980), pp. 161–63.

2. Ibid. pp. 219–28, where Metz clearly emphasizes the positive dimensions of Rahner's spiritual and intellectual performance.

3. Ibid., pp. 60–73.

4. Cf. Lonergan, *Method in Theology* (New York: Herder and Herder, 1972), p. 140.

5. A Gouldner, *The Two Marxisms: Contradictions and Anomalies in the Development of Theory* (New York: The Seabury Press, 1980), pp. 177–98; see also pp. 8–37. L. Kolakowski, *Main Currents of Marxism, The Founders* (Oxford: Clarendon Press, 1978), vol. 1. D. McLellan, *Marx Before Marxism* (New York: Harper & Row, 1970).

6. Cf. J. O'Malley's "Introduction" to his translation of Marx's *Critique of Hegel's "Philosophy of Right"* (Cambridge: The University Press, 1970), pp. ix–lxiii. Cf., for example, Marx's early poem on Hegel in K. Marx and F. Engels, *Collected Works* (New York: International Publishers, 1975), vol. 1, pp. 576f.:

> *Kant and Fichte soar to heavens blue*
> *Seeking for some distant land,*
> *I but seek to grasp profound and true*
> *That which—in the street I find.*

with his analysis in *The German Ideology* of how Kant's critique of practical reason fully reflects the contradictions of political liberalism, *Collected Works* (New York: International Publishers, 1976), vol. 5, pp. 193–96; and his remarks on Hegel's dialectics in the "Afterword to the Second German Edition" of his *Capital* (New York: International Publishers, 1967), pp. 19f.

7. On the praxis enlightenment, cf. the previous chap., also M. Lamb., "Theology and Praxis: A Response (II) to Bernard Lonergan," *Catholic Theological Society of America Proceedings* 32 (1977): 22–30.

8. Cf. G. Baum, *Religion and Alienation* (New York: Paulist Press, 1975), pp. 21–61; also chap. 2 of this book.

9. Cf. W. Oelmüller, *Die Unbefriedigte Aufklärung: Beiträge zu einer Theorie der Moderne von Lessing, Kant und Hegel* (Frankfurt: Suhrkamp, 1969); O. Schwemmer, *Philosophie der Praxis: Versuch zur Grundlegung einer Lehre vom moralischen Argumentieren in Verbindung mit einer Interpretattion der praktischen Philosophie Kants* (Frankfurt: Suhrkamp, 1971); M. Riedel, *Theorie und Praxis im Denken Hegels* (Stuttgart: Kohlhammer, 1965); M. Theunissen, *Hegels Lehre vom absoluten Geist als theologisch-politischer Traktat* (Berlin: de Gruyter, 1970); C. Taylor, *Hegel* (New York: Cambridge Univer-

sity Press, 1975), pp. 510–33; W. Becker, *Hegels Begriff der Dialektik und das Prinzip des Idealismus* (Stuttgart: Kohlhammer, 1969).

10. K. Löwith, *From Hegel to Nietzsche: The Revolution in Nineteenth Century Thought*, trans. D. Green (New York: Doubleday Anchor Books, 1967), pp. 50–134; M. Xhaufflaire, *Feuerbach et la théologie de la sécularisation* (Paris: Les éditions du Cerf, 1970).

11. L. Feuerbach, *Anthropologischer Materialismus: Ausgewählte Schriften*, 2 vols., ed. and introduced by A. Schmidt (Frankfurt: Europäische Verlaganstalt, 1967), esp. vol. 1, pp. 5–64, 75–162.

12. D. Easton and K. Guddat (eds.), *Writings of the Young Marx on Philosophy and Society* (New York: Doubleday Anchor Books, 1967), p. 95. S. Avineri, *The Social and Political Thought of Karl Marx* (New York: Cambridge University Press, 1968), pp. 8–40, 124–49.

13. J. O'Malley, "Marx, Marxism and Method," in S. Avineri (ed.), *The Varieties of Marxism* (The Hague: Martinus Nijhof, 1977), pp. 7–41.

14. Ibid., pp. 18–25.

15. Ibid., pp. 25f., 40–41.

16. Gouldner, op. cit., pp. 32–63, 289–389.

17. M. Lamb, "The Exigencies of Meaning and Metascience," in T. Dunne and J. M. Laporte (eds.) *Trinification of the World: A Festschrift in Honor of Frederick Crowe* (Toronto: Regis College Press, 1978), pp. 15–45; H. Peukert, *Wissenschaftstheorie-Handlungstheorie-Fundamentale Theologie* (Frankfurt: Suhrkamp, 1978), pp. 229–300.

18. M. Gross, *The Psychological Society* (New York: Simon and Schuster, 1978); T. Bottomore and R. Nisbet (eds.), *A History of Sociological Analysis* (New York: Basic Books, 1978), pp. 237–86, 321–61, 457–98, 557–98; E. Wilson and M. Harris, "The Envelope and the Twig," *The Sciences* 18 (1978): 10–15, 27.

19. C. Davis, "The Reconvergence of Theology and Religious Studies," *Studies in Religion* 4/3 (1974–75): 205–21; and the five responses to this study in ibid., pp. 222–35. G. Sauter, *Vor einem neuen Methodenstreit in der Theologie?* (Munich: Kaiser, 1970); D. Kelsey, *The Uses of Scripture in Recent Theology* (Philadelphia: Fortress Press, 1975); V. Harvey, *The Historian and the Believer* (New York: Macmillan, 1966).

20. P. Eicher, *Die Anthropologische Wende* (Freiburg: Universitätsverlag, 1970), pp. 13–33.; F. Fiorenza, "Introduction: Karl Rahner and the Kantian Problematic," in K. Rahner, *Spirit in the World*, trans. W. Dych (New York: Herder and Herder, 1968), pp. xix–xlv; A. Carr, *The Theological Method of Karl Rahner* (Missoula: Scholars Press, 1977).

21. Eicher, op. cit., pp. 115–99; Carr, op. cit., pp. 59–123.

22. V. Sülbeck, *Neomarxismus und Theologie: Gesellschaftskritik in*

*Kritischer Theorie und Politischer Theologie* (Freiburg: Herder, 1977); R. Johns, *Man in the World: The Theology of Johannes B. Metz* (Missoula: Scholars Press, 1976); M. Xhaufflaire (ed.), *La pratique de la théologie politique* (Tournai: Casterman, 1974).

23. J. B. Metz, *Faith in History and Society*, pp. 154–68; also Metz's "An Identity Crisis in Christianity? Transcendental and Political Responses," in W. Kelly (ed.), *Discovery and Theology: Studies in Honor of Karl Rahner* (Milwaukee: Marquette University Press, 1980), pp. 121–41; also the responses to Metz's study by Tracy and Lamb in ibid., pp. 142–51.

24. Johns, op. cit., pp. 132–49; M. Lamb, *History, Method and Theology* (Missoula: Scholars Press, 1978), pp. 1–54.

25. B. Lonergan, *Verbum: Word and Idea in Aquinas*, ed. D. Burrell (Notre Dame: University Press, 1967), pp. vii–xv, 1–95; D. Tracy, *The Achievement of Bernard Lonergan* (New York: Herder and Herder, 1970), pp. 45–103.

26. B. Lonergan, *Insight: A Study of Human Understanding* (New York: Harper & Row, 1978), pp. 3–172.

27. Ibid., pp. 207–44; Lamb, *History, Method and Theology*, pp. 254–81. Lonergan developed a strong critique of bureaucracy as illustrative of sin in the social process in his unpublished *Lectures on the Philosophy of Education* (Cincinnati: Xavier University, 1959), lecture 3, pp. 10–13.

28. *Insight*, pp. 103–39, 607–33; Lamb, *History, Method and Theology*, pp. 480–85.

29. Lamb, *History, Method and Theology*, pp. 56–93.

30. G. Sala, *Das Apriori in der menschlichen Erkenntnis* (Meisenheim: Verlag Anton Hain, 1972), pp. 41–68, 297–389.

31. J. Nilson, *Hegel's Phenomenology and Lonergan's Insight* (Meisenheim: Verlag Anton Hain, 1980).

32. W. Loewe, "Dialectics of Sin: Lonergan's Insight and the Critical Theory of Max Horkheimer," *Anglican Theological Review* 41/2 (1979): 224–45.

33. B. Lonergan, *Collection*, ed. F. Crowe (New York: Herder and Herder, 1967), pp. 198–220.

34. Lamb, *History, Method and Theology*, pp. 254–72, 424–48.

35. *Insight*, p. xxviii.

36. B. Lonergan, *Method in Theology* (New York: Herder and Herder, 1972), pp. 39f.

37. B. Lonergan, "The Ongoing Genesis of Methods," *Studies in Religion* 6/4 (1977): 341–55; here 341 and 351.

38. Ibid., p. 349.

39. *Insight*, pp. 469–82, 530ff.; *Method in Theology*, pp. 27–55, 235–66. On the significance of this shift to a generalized empirical method which emphasizes the dialectics of the human good, cf. R.

Doran, *Subject and Psyche: Ricoeur, Jung and the Search for Foundations* (Washington, D.C.: University Press of America, 1977), pp. 17–113; also his "Theological Grounds for a World-Cultural Humanity," in M. Lamb (ed.), *Creativity and Method: Essays in Honor of Bernard Lonergan* (Milwaukee: Marquette University Press, 1981) pp. 105–22.

40. Lonergan, "The Ongoing Genesis of Methods," pp. 348–52.

41. Doran, *Subject and Psyche*, pp. 253–309; Lamb, *History, Method and Theology*, pp. 422–53.

42. Lonergan, "The Ongoing Genesis of Methods," pp. 345 and 348:

> ... privacy in the world mediated by meaning has to be contrived and defended and even then it is limited. In that world one is taught by others and, for the most part, what they know they have learnt from others, in an ongoing process that stretches back over millennia.... None of us is an Adam living at the origin of human affairs, becoming all that he is by his own decisions, and learning all that he knows by personal experience, personal insight, personal discernment. We are products of a process that in its several aspects is named socialization, acculturation, education.

All human persons are intrinsically related to other human persons. Both the personhood question (Who are we?) and the nature question (What are we?) can only be answered in relation to the ongoing processes of human history. But where the nature question admits of explanatory understanding in terms of the universe of emergent probability, the personhood question admits of narrative-symbolic understanding heuristically oriented into mystery.

43. Ibid., p. 345.

44. Lonergan, "Sacralization and Secularization" (1974, n.p.), p. 24.

45. M. Weber, *Economy and Society: An Outline of Interpretative Sociology*, ed. G. Roth and C. Wittich (Berkeley: University of California Press, 1978), vol. 2, pp. 956–1003; M. Weber, *The Protestant Ethic and the Spirit of Capitalism* trans. T. Parsons (New York: C. Scribner's Sons, 1958), pp. 155–84; G. Baum, *Religion and Alienation*, pp. 162–92; D. Martin, *A General Theory of Secularization* (New York: Harper & Row, 1978).

46. Lamb, "The Challenge of Critical Theory," pp. 205–08.

47. *Method in Theology*, pp. 27–55, 108–12.

48. Gouldner, *The Two Marxisms*, pp. 3–31.

49. Ibid., pp. 32–79.

50. Ibid., pp. 155–63 and references given there.

51. *Insight*, pp. 86–102, 115–139, 259–62, 458–83, 607–18.

52. *Method in Theology*, pp. 36–47; Lamb, *History, Method and Theology*, pp. 388–441.

53. Lonergan, "The Ongoing Genesis of Method," pp. 348–52.

54. *History, Method and Theology*, pp. 195–209; also J. Raymaker, "The Theory and Praxis of Social Ethics," in Lamb (ed.), *Creativity and Method*, pp. 339–52.

55. Lamb, *History, Method and Theology*, pp. 156–209, and the references given there.

56. Adorno, *Über Walter Benjamin* (Frankfurt: Suhrkamp, 1970), p. 117.

57. Lonergan, "An Essay in Circulation Analysis" (Boston College, 1978–80, n.p.), p. 2. "In other words, the productive process itself contains implicit criteria, and if these criteria are unknown or ignored, things may go from bad to worse. And as we all know, such an eventuality has already occurred." Also P. McShane, "Lonergan and the Actual Contexts of Economics," in Lamb (ed.), *Creativity and Method* pp. 556–70; also M. Gibbons, "Insight and Emergence: An Introduction to Lonergan's Circulation Analysis," ibid., pp. 529–41; J. Schumpeter, *History of Economic Analysis*, (New York: Oxford University Press, 1974), pp. v–xiii, 1–1260.

58. Lonergan, *An Essay in Circulation Analysis*, p. 2.

59. Cf. J. Segundo, "Capitalism versus Socialism: Crux Theologica" in R. Gibellini (ed.), *Frontiers of Theology in Latin America* (Maryknoll: Orbis Books, 1979), pp. 240–59; G. Baum, *The Social Imperative* (New York: Paulist Press, 1979), pp. 3–38, 70–98.

60. M. Lamb, "The Production Process and Exponential Growth: A Study in Socio-Economics and Theology," in F. Lawrence (ed.), *Lonergan Workshop* (Missoula: Scholars Press, 1978), vol. 1, pp. 257–307; also chap. 2 of this book.

61. Lonergan, *An Essay in Circulation Analysis*, pp. 70–107. For illustrations of the misadventures of the multinational corporations, Lonergan draws primarily upon R. Barnet and R. Müller, *Global Reach: The Power of the Multinational Corporations* (New York: Simon and Schuster, 1974).

62. For a descriptive account of some of these sufferings, cf. P. Lernoux, *Cry of the People* (New York: Doubleday, 1980); also S. George, *How the Other Half Dies: the Real Reasons for World Hunger* (Montclair: Allanheld, Osmun and Co., 1977); F. Lappé and J. Collins, *Food First: Beyond the Myth of Scarcity*, rev. ed. (New York: Ballantine Books, 1979) and Lonergan's review of the first edition of this book, *Theological Studies* 39/1 (1978): 198f. Also Jack A. Nelson, *Hunger For Justice* (Maryknoll: Orbis, 1980).

63. Lonergan, "A New Pastoral Theology" (lecture, 1973, n.p.), p. 22. "Theology and Praxis," *Catholic Theological Society of America Proceedings* 32 (1977): pp. 1–16; also the responses by E. Braxton and M. Lamb in ibid., pp. 17–30. On how Lonergan's theological method acknowledges that "orthopraxis has a value beyond orthodoxy," cf.

Lonergan, "Mission and Spirit," *Concilium* 9/10 (London: Burns and Oats, 1974), pp. 69–78, here 75.

64. *Method in Theology*, pp. 105–07, 237–44, 267–71.

65. Lonergan, "Mission and Spirit," pp. 69–78; also his "Healing and Creating in History," in *Bernard Lonergan: Three Lectures* (Montreal: Thomas More Institute, 1975), pp. 55–68.

66. *Method in Theology*, pp. 85–99.

67. Lonergan, "The Ongoing Genesis of Methods," p. 353.

68. Ibid., pp. 354–55.

69. Ibid., p. 354.

70. Ibid.

71. Ibid., pp. 351–52.

72. Cf. chap. 3 of this book.

73. Lonergan, "The Dehellenization of Dogma," in his *A Second Collection*, ed. W. Ryan and B. Tyrrell (Philadelphia: Westminster Press, 1974), pp. 11–32; W. Kümmel, *The New Testament: The History of the Investigation of Problems*, trans. S. Gilmour and H. Kee (Nashville: Abingdon Press, 1972), pp. 120–308; A von Harnack, *Lehrbuch der Dogmengeschichte*, 2 vols., reprinted from the 4 ed. (Darmstadt: Wissenschaftliche Buchgesellschaft, 1964), vol. 1, pp. 496–796.

74. Q. Quesnell, "Beliefs and Authenticity," in M. Lamb (ed.), *Creativity and Method*, pp. 173–183. On Kantian secular moral religiosity, cf. Immanuel Kant, *Religion Within the Limits of Reason Alone*, trans. T. Greene and H. Hudson (New York: Harper Torchbooks, 1960); A. Wood, *Kant's Moral Religion* (Ithaca: Cornell University Press, 1970); on the neo-Kantian Ritschlians, cf. D. Mueller, *An Introduction to the Theology of A. Ritschl* (Philadelphia: Westminster Press, 1969).

75. N. Gottwald, *The Tribes of Yahweh* (Maryknoll: Orbis Books, 1979); note how Lonergan's critical realism is capable of sublating both the idealism and cultural materialism alternatives Gottwald operates within. G. Theissen, *Urchristliche Wundergeschichten* (Göttingen: Gütersloher Verlaghaus G. Mohn, 1974); P. Trible, *God and the Rhetoric of Sexuality* (Philadelphia: Fortress Press, 1978); R. Cassidy, *Jesus, Politics and Society: A Study of Luke's Gospel* (Maryknoll: Orbis Books, 1978); B. Meyer, *The Aims of Jesus* (London: SCM Press, 1979).

76. On the debates the social-critical approaches are occasioning, cf. J. Gager's review essay of recent books by R. Grant, A. Malherbe, and G. Theissen in *Religious Studies Review* 5/3 (1979): 174–80. Also L. Cormie, "The Hermeneutical Privilege of the Oppressed," *Catholic Theological Society of America Proceedings* 33 (1978): 155–81; and D. Harrington, "Sociological Concepts of the Early Church," *Theological Studies* 41 (1980): 181–90.

77. W. Loewe, "Lonergan and the Law of the Cross," *Anglican Theological Review* 59 (1977): 162–74; also Loewe's as yet unpublished dissertation, "Toward the Critical Mediation of Theology: A Development of the Soteriological Theme in the Work of B. Lonergan" (Marquette University, Milwaukee, 1974). Also the reference in n. 32 above.

78. Lonergan, *The Way to Nicea: The Dialectical Development of Trinitarian Theology*, trans. C. O'Donovan (Philadelphia: Westminster Press, 1976); Lonergan, "The Origins of Christian Realism," in his *A Second Collection*, pp. 239–61.

79. *The Way to Nicea*, p. viii. Remember that the experiment of generalized empirical method "is conducted not by any individual, not by any generation, but by the historical process itself." Lonergan, "The Ongoing Genesis of Methods," p. 345.

80. *The Way to Nicea*, pp. 105–37, *Method in Theology*, pp. 305–18.

81. *The Way to Nicea*, pp. vii–viii.

82. There is, of course, a critical complementarity between historical and dialectical analyses, as Lonergan brings out in his functional specialties of how research, interpretation, and history provide results for dialectics, cf. *Method in Theology*, pp. 125–45, 235ff.

83. R. Haughton, *The Catholic Thing* (Springfield: Templegate, 1979), p. 17. Note how Haughton's narrative reconstructions here are dialectically oriented to orthopraxis in the present for the sake of the future. On how such an orientation is constitutive of political theology, cf. Lamb, *History, Method and Theology*, pp. 30–53. For another recent study of this aspect of Catholicism, cf. E. Braxton, *The Wisdom Community* (New York: Paulist Press, 1980). Braxton acknowledges: "Indeed, much of the dynamic of this book can be understood as an attempt to translate and apply many of the methodological insights of Lonergan and Tracy into a pastoral context." Ibid., p. viii.

84. Cf. references in n. 76 above. Also the articles in *Concilium* on neo-Conservatism, ed. G. Baum, esp. M. Fleet, "Neo-Conservatism in Latin America." Also A. Hennelly, *Theologies in Conflict: The Challenge of Juan L. Segundo* (Maryknoll: Orbis Books, 1979); R. Brown, *Theology in a New Key: Responding to Liberation Themes* (Philadelphia: Westminster Press, 1978).

85. Cf. Hans Küng and Johann B. Metz, "Perspektiven für eine Kirche der Zukunft," *Publik-Forum* 9/13 (June 1980): 15–21. Also R. Siebert, "The Church from Below: Küng & Metz," in *Cross Currents* 31/1 (1981): 62–84.

86. A. Schindler (ed.), *Monotheismus als politisches Problem? Erik Peterson und die Kritik der politischen Theologie* (Gütersloh: G. Mohn, 1978).

87. Besides the references in n. 84 above, cf. S. Ogden, *Faith and Freedom: Toward a Theology of Liberation* (Nashville: Abingdon

Press, 1979), pp. 33–37, 44–65, 115–24. Ogden's criticism of liberation theologies for not engaging in critical reflection cannot be sustained in the light of the untranslated methodological works, cf. note 92 of chapter 3 above.

88. For example, D. Keefe, "Sacramental Sexuality and the Ordination of Women," *Communio* 5 (1978): 228–51; also his "The Ordination of Women," *New Oxford Review* 47/1 (1980): 12–14.

89. Cf. Meyer, *The Aims of Jesus*, pp. 13–110, on the hermeneutical issues involved in the historical-critical quest for the historical Jesus. Also Lamb, *History, Method and Theology*, pp. 41–93, 518–30. An adequate social-critical reconstruction of historical criticism has yet to be written. Note, however, G. Bauer, *Geschichtlichkeit: Wege und Irrwege eines Begriffs* (Berlin: de Gruyter, 1963); and L. von Renthe-Fink, *Geschichtlichkeit* (Göttingen: Vandenhoeck und Ruprecht, 1968) and H. Baumgartner, *Kontinutät und Geschichte: zur Kritik und Metakritik der historischen Vernunft* (Frankfurt: Suhrkamp, 1972).

90. Besides the references in n. 7 and 9 above, cf. K.-O. Apel, *Towards a Transformation of Philosophy*, trans. G. Adey and D. Frisby (Boston: Routledge and Kegan Paul, 1980), pp. 136–79, 225–300; and the theological critique and retrieval of Apel by H. Peukert, *Wissenschaftstheorie-Handlungstheorie-Fundamentale Theologie*, pp. 300–55. Also M. Lamb, "Contemporary Education and Sinful Social Structures," to appear in a forthcoming issue of *Lonergan Workshop*.

91. *Method in Theology*, p. 319.

92. Besides the references in n. 78 and 86 above, cf. E. Schüssler Fiorenza, "Feminist Theology as a Critical Theology of Liberation," *Theological Studies* 36 (1975): 605–26; and "You are not to be called Father: Early Christian History in a Feminist Perspective," *Cross Currents* 29 (1979): 301–23.

93. E. Peterson, "Monotheismus als politisches Problem" and "Christus als Imperator" in *Theologische Traktate* (Munich: Kösel, 1951), pp. 45–147, 150–64; F. Fiorenza, "Critical Social Theory and Christology," *Catholic Theological Society of America Proceedings* 30 (1975): pp. 63–110.

94. Q. Quesnell, "Beliefs and Authenticity," as in n. 74 above. Theologians who try to legitimate the exclusion of women from ministry (cf. n. 88 above) by claiming that males sacramentally symbolize transcendence and females sacramentally symbolize immanence fail, because of their naive empiricism, to live up to the critical realist values expressed in classical orthodoxy—as though we could know the personalizing orientations of transcendence and immanence by taking a good look at the already-out-there-now-real. Such a naive empiricist stance also overlooks the dialectics of sociosexual value conflicts in the Christian traditions. Cf. John Boswell, *Christianity,*

*Social Tolerance, and Homosexuality* (Chicago: Univ. of Chicago Press, 1980) and Joan Morris, *The Lady was a Bishop* (New York: Macmillan, 1973). Morris has recently completed important research, for example, on how Athanasius, whom Lonergan identifies as a critical realist, had a more positive evaluation of sexuality in marriage, and how Athanasius might possibly have recognized a practice of Christian virgins celebrating the eucharist together.

95. "The Production Process and Exponential Growth," pp. 284–97.

96. M. O'Callaghan, "Rahner and Lonergan on Foundational Theology," in M. Lamb (ed.), *Creativity and Method*, pp. 123–140.

97. Cf. Eicher, op. cit., pp. 125–34, 153–71; also the references given in n. 23 above. For the two levels of reflection in Rahner's theology, cf. his *Foundations of Christian Faith*, trans. W. Dych (New York: Seabury Press, 1978), pp. 8–21.

98. K. Jaspers, *Philosophy and the World: Selected Essays and Lectures* (Chicago: Henry Regnery Co., 1963), p. 22.

# Index of Names